EYES OF INNOCENCE

By

Sherry Jo Saunders

ISBN: 1-4033-4721-2 (e-book)
ISBN: 1-4033-4722-0 (Paperback)

Library of Congress Control Number: 2002092826

This book is printed on acid free paper.

Printed in the United States of America
Bloomington, IN

1stBooks - rev. 07/16/03

This book is dedicated to:

My Husband, Rand,
and
the three extensions
of my body and soul:

Shannon
Chance
Duran

Loved and always needed are:

Kaylee Ann & Christie,
given to me through Shannon's Love
P.J.
Sie
Mine a Pee
Munchkin
Sunshine
Tweetie
Flo with Alice

Appreciation for humoring me:

Haughty
Johnson
B.B.
Darryloo, Killer & Kody Bear, too
Jake & Patsy
Jim & Ila

Introduction

Situated along the vast Gulf of Mexico lies a land in which the people who inhabit the area are as colorful as the history in which they were born. A land that to this day time has resisted change in order to ensure its inhabitants of their culture. A culture steadfastly held onto, selfishly.

It is a place the United States offered no resistance to when Spain relinquished its hold to France. A place without much hope of ever amounting to anything save for its wildlife resources that produced a lucrative fur trade and abundance of fisheries.

In an effort to please his King, Robert Cavalier of France, claimed the area and named it after his monarch, Louis XIV.

LOUISIANA

The fur trade was at first presumed to be the land's strongest resource, offering muskrat, mink, otter, raccoon and opossum. As time passed cotton emerged as another strong commodity and slaves were transported into the area to work the large fields.

The slaves were not looked down upon so much by the inhabitants of the area for they, too, were of different descendents. The French people of Arcadia had long since invaded this peaceful land in hopes of building a future for themselves. To achieve this new life, they thought nothing of blending with Spanish and Indian. Then, later, with the beautiful people from the Guinea coast of Africa.

Each mix brought with them a fusing of beliefs and religion. Among all, however, religion was the strongest belief instilled in all. The belief in baptism was paramount. As long as a person was baptized, and their name registered with the local church, they were Christians. Children of God.

Baptism was revered throughout the land and there was never any notice taken when the church pews were filled with white, red, olive or dark skinned worshippers.

The mixed bloodlines gave forth children struggling with the different languages until the language became a blend of syllables now referred to as a Cajun dialect.

Prejudice came later with time as the earth began to yield new riches. First to crystallize was sugar from the cane fields, then an abundance of oil gushed forth from beneath the soil.

The cotton owners, sugar cane farmers and oil merchants soon separated themselves from the everyday local folks still struggling to make a living. These home grown people were, more or less, the ones who had remained close to the life in which they were accustomed. The fisheries. For though there had been those who had chosen a different future, the fishing industry was as constant and demanding as any other. These people just did not create great wealth from their goods of shrimp, oysters, and fish. Certainly, they did not compare to the riches amassed from cotton and sugar farming and especially from oil drilling.

Progress was soon defined as civilization. And, this new civilization separated the rich from the poor.

The thinking man from the doer. Thus came prejudice. Hate.

The once peaceful bounty of land soon became a land of selfish interest and the greed for money. The color of skin promoted or demoted one's future. After acquisition of the territory by President Thomas Jefferson through his Louisiana Purchase, children were punished in school for any use of a language spoken other than English. Only in their own homes did they have the freedom to speak as their father's had spoken before them.

Still the Cajun dialect has survived to this day. And though there are different uses of words, depending on the area, the people still hold fast to what they have inherited.

Prologue

CYPRESS, LOUISIANA

JUNE, 1949

The beautiful, star-filled clear sky was a sharp contrast to the event taking place below. The malicious act had started off as merely a dare. A contest of young male pride. A game.

Screams from a young girl's torture, silenced the usual cries from the swamp frogs.

It was as if all the creatures of the swamp hushed, in an effort to allow the stranger's cries to be heard.

Nis struggled against her assailants, screaming, biting, kicking, but her struggles were useless against the three young men. She could smell the strong stench emanating from them as they talked amongst themselves.

"All right buddy. Let's see if you're the man you claim to be! We have her. Go ahead."

Fourteen-year-old Nis tried to free her arms from the two assailants only to find herself held even tighter. She stopped struggling for a moment to try and think. She had been jumped from behind and now, as she was forced down on the damp cool earth, she raised her head to see her attackers.

The face looming over her was not an unknown face. Clear eyes met dark eyes and for a moment he hesitated.

"Non! Qui tu veux?" Nis asked just before the scream erupted from her throat as she felt the first thrust from the attacker.

"Hurry up, man," came an urgent plea from one of the other attackers.

Stan heard Fred's voice just before he reached his climax. "Ahhhhh!" he screamed, shuddering from the release.

Breathing hard, he stood. Looking down at the girl as he hastily buckled his trouser, he suddenly felt sick. His head began to clear through the cloud of intoxication and the realization of what had just occurred hit him. Hard!

Her face had been a blur up until now. Pieces of how they had gotten to this God-forsaken place began to emerge.

It had been a joke! A dare. They had come out here to buy some of Old Uncle John's "Corn Water", so-called by the locals because of its potent blend of corn and other mysterious ingredients. Everybody around knew where to get the stuff.

They had spotted the girl walking away from the house as Old Uncle John left them to retrieve a jug. Each of them took a note of her lush, long, black hair and the way she glided through the forest like a seductive breeze.

It was after they had left and started passing the jug around that Fred spoke up. "That Uncle John's niece sure is a fine piece. Yessiree, she ought to be around...Mmmm eighteen years old by now, don't you think, fellas?"

"Naw, can't be that old," Sly said as he drove down the narrow, dirt lane. Barely wide enough for a horse drawn cart, let alone his '46 Chevy Roadster.

"How old do you think she is?" Stan asked before taking another swig and wiping his mouth on the back of his sleeve.

Sly was quiet for a moment, his face contorted as he strained to remember the girl. "She's almost gotta be at least seventeen by now."

"Think so?" Stan queried.

"At least!" Sly stated, matter-of-factly as the heavy brown earthen jug was passed to him. "God, but that's some strong stuff," he exclaimed, leaving his friends to ponder whether he was talking about the girl or the hooch.

Fred laughed, reaching for the jug. "This night is for celebrating! Come on, guys, soon we can kiss ol'Mcnally High away!"

The hoots and yells from the small sports car went unnoticed as they sped off down the long curvy isolated road. As agreed upon by all three young graduates, this night was to be a night they would all remember.

Chapter One

Nis had glanced back at the three young men as she walked barefoot, into the woods. She hummed softly as she strode on the well-worn path to the small, slanted building. The outhouse was only about two hundred yards from the house, but it was obscured by the thick foliage and wide girths of the trees. She really did not need to answer nature's call, she mostly wanted to get out of sight when she saw the car pull up. Nis was well aware of how her uncle made his living and was quite used to being awaken at any hour of the night as people as far away as Baton Rouge came to buy Uncle John's smooth Corn Water. She knew all too well to stay out of sight and not underfoot when 'business' was going on. She had never been allowed to speak to anyone, save for the Treater, Eileen.

Leaning back on the side of the outhouse she reflected on the three young men. Though she did not know them personally, she had certainly seen them around. There was that Fred Long of whom she thought resembled a swollen toad, he was so fat. His Father owned the hardware store in Cypress and though there had been only a few times when she was allowed to accompany Uncle John into town she took notice of everything. Fred worked for his father after school and to Nis's young mind he always stared at her strangely. Though truth be told, she admitted to herself, everyone stared at her strangely.

Then there was that other guy, Sly. She did not remember seeing him before a couple of years ago. He

1

was not a local. Someone once commented to Uncle John that Sly's dad was the one who had bought the waterfront property at the edge of town to build boats. "The man's makin' a damn good livin' from that business," she remembered him telling her uncle, though the man's language was a little different from the one she spoke, as it was with most of the people in the area.

And last, but not least, in her eyes anyway, was Stan Peterson. To her young mind he was the most beautiful of all creatures. His hair was as golden as the sun. His skin was light. Everything about him was bright except his eyes. His eyes were the color of a fawn's. Soft. Kind. Dark.

"Not like mine." she thought to herself. Too many were the times to count when her uncle refused to look at her because of her eyes. "Non yeaux" he would say, shaking his head, sadly. 'No eyes.'

That is why people stared at her, she thought to herself.

She listened as the car the young men were in sped away. Feeling that it was safe enough to return, she made her way back to the decrepit, cedar shingled cottage.

Uncle John was nowhere to be seen, but she knew exactly where he was. Down at the 'knees' checking on his new batch of brew. "Le genous", as Uncle John referred the place, was a desolate cluster of cedar stumps surrounded by a treacherous expanse in the bayou know locally as "bogs".

Unless you knew each step to take in that direction it would certainly prove to be fatal as only Nis and her Uncle knew where the 'bogs' were located. The Bogs were nothing but soft sand without, as far as anyone knew, a bottom. Surrounded by a thicket of tall cypress trees dripping with Spanish moss and the ever-multiplying cypress 'knees'. Just one step, misplaced, would present a slow agonizing death. It proved to be a perfect hiding place for their only means of support.

Her chore of the last picking of the dried corn stored away in the large, burlap bags for Uncle John's future brew now behind her, Nis reached below the rust-stained porcelain sink for a large pot. She then retrieved the tightly wrapped package of pig feet from the cooler. The firewood was neatly stacked close by and within a few moments she had the pot filled with water from the aging sink pipe, connected to the cistern on the roof, on the wood-burning stove. Uncle John always expected her to cook. Whether he was sober enough to eat or not, she knew to have him something on hand to fill his bloated belly.

It was seldom he went into town to retrieve anything they needed. Most often it was someone coming by to barter their goods for Uncle John's stupor-inducing concoction. Such was the case with the pig feet. Cypress town's butcher, a rotund, affable sort, had ventured out from town earlier in the day.

Evening was now setting in. Nis loved this time of day. Always sure her chores were done, she reveled in the sun easing down below the tree line, casting a rainbow of colors off the dark, damp, thickness of the swamp. Most times she sat on the porch step to watch evening roll in but tonight she thought she would just walk along the lane.

She was no stranger to these foreboding woods. No stranger to any of the sounds of the night.

Listening to the awakening frogs she smiled to herself and began to hum. She loved to sing, but knew the words to so few songs. Most times she just hummed.

The cart-path lane that led out to the paved road was miles long. As always, she felt safe, protected by the thickly grown cypress trees that lined the roadway on both sides. In fact, should two cars coming in opposite directions try to pass, it would be impossible. The only intruder would be someone coming to see Uncle John, and the times that that had occurred, she was always able to hear the roar of the engine in plenty of time to hide in the brush. Out of anyone's sight.

The evening drew chilly as the all-consuming blackness of night closed in. It was a cloudless evening and the newly risen moon was giving off just enough light to help guide her as she started back toward the cottage. She could see the amber glow emanating from the lantern in her house. It appeared welcoming.

It was her last peaceful moment, she would later remember. Suddenly she was grabbed. In an instant, a hand was placed roughly over her mouth to still her cries as she was pulled from the road into the woods.

She could smell the whiskey and tried in vain to free her mouth, but it was only after she was thrown to the ground and her arms pinned down that her attackers released the pressure on her lips. Then, she screamed.

The assault only lasted moments, but to Nis's mind the torture lasted a lifetime. Never had she been touched as the young boy had touched her, and though she begged them to stop and even managed to ask, why, they seemed oblivious to her cries. Her long hair was being pulled as one of her assailants had his knee on it, and try as she might, she could not stop the madness taking place.

Suddenly, the scorching pain thrust into her young body caused her to almost convulse. A dizziness engulfed her and she gladly allowed herself to sink into the dark hollowness of it.

Stan stood, his knees stinging from the onslaught of the dried twigs that had gouged him with his every thrust. Without thinking he bent over to rub away some of the soreness. The excitement of the last few hours combined with the strong liquor almost made him reel forward.

"Whoa, man!" Fred exclaimed with an evil chuckle. "You can't pass out on us now! Me and Sly wanna have a go at this beauty!"

Stan look to Fred then to Sly. They each had a strange look in their glowing eyes. Hunger?

Just then, Sly stood up releasing his hold on the lifeless form. "My God! She's dead." His voice cracked.

Stan stared down at the girl. The moon cast an eerie glow on her face. Her eyes were wide open. Staring, unseeing, colorless eyes.

Without another word, Sly took off running in the direction of the old roadster. Fred was soon jolted into following him as Stan stood, looking down at the beautiful, slim, girl. Her legs remained spread apart, debris covering parts of her white, smooth thighs.

Nausea erupted. It was a moment before Stan was able to catch his breath after loosing the contents of his stomach. Wiping his mouth with the back of his hand, he said softly to the ghostly, white face. "It was a dare.

I never meant to..." Tears choked off his words as he heard his name being called off in the distance. Realizing it to be Fred's voice he turned to run. As if the devil himself was on his heels, he ran, sobbing loudly.

THREE DAYS LATER

Ring ~~~~~"Hello, Stan?"

"Yeah."

"Heard anything?"

"No." came the short reply. "You?"

"No, man. Nothing." Silence. "Later then."

"Yeah, later." Click.

"Stanley?" His Mother called from the foot of the stairs. "Are you ready? We don't want to be late." She chided gently. He reached for the bag on his bed that held the black robe and a change of clothing.

"Coming Mother." He replied, as if in a daze.

Slowly he descended the staircase looking into his mother's soft brown eyes.

Suddenly, she became concerned. "Are you all right? You seem a little pale, Dear?"

"I'm fine Mother." He answered mechanically.

"My, I never thought you would be nervous," she said teasingly. "You have waited for this moment for a long time. In just a few months you can leave this small, dusty, backwater town, as you have always described it. You will be going to college!" With that said, Janie Peterson ushered her son out the front door and into their awaiting chauffeur-driven sedan.

She addressed the driver: "Let's get this nervous young graduate to the school before he changes his mind," she joked. Then, as she began putting on her long, white gloves she turned to look into her son's eyes and said, "Relax. One day you will look back on this time as the happiest of your life!"

Stan heard her words, but deep in the pit of his stomach, he knew he would remember this time as anything but the happiest in his life.

Chapter Two

MARCH, 1950

Nis listened as her uncle spoke to the man outside. Her room was adjacent to the long front porch and her window was slightly opened to allow in some of the early spring air. The winter had been severely cold. Long shivering days and nights had kept her shut up inside. It was a blessed change to open a window and smell the sweet aroma of spring.

She lay in her bed, listening as the customer drove off. Relieved, she let out a heavy sigh. The pains were coming quickly now and it would not do to have made any noises while Uncle John was "doin' business." He was never to be interrupted by her. Never. That is why she always took herself away from the house. But tonight she could not. She had tried to walk, only to have a stream of water flow down her legs. God, but she hurt all over!

Minutes could have been hours. She had no idea. She was frightened beyond understanding as wave after wave of pain coursed through her young body.

Eileen, the Treater, had been by a few weeks earlier and had tried to help the young girl to understand the strange transformation in her body. She knew to speak to the young girl in 'le francais de meche'. (Marsh French).

Eileen explained how very soon Nis would bear a be'be. She also told her she would try to be close by when the time came.

Although Nis understood the Treaters' words, she knew nothing about how this had came to be. Confused, frightened she carried the heavy child growing within her and continued on with her life as she knew it. But, now, it seemed her body would burst from this be'be wanting out.

Old John entered the house noting that the lantern had not been lit. With the sun going down, you could barely see inside the room. Then, Old John noticed the absence of the smell of food cooking on the black iron stove.

Before his jumbled mind could come together with reasoning, the hair stood up on the back of his neck. The scream he heard was bone-chilling. Only in a near death situation had he heard such an anguished cry of the soul. He had seen many deaths during the war, and that last cry coming from Nis's room, was the sound a soul made when the choice was no longer theirs to live or die. It was a sound that still haunted him to this day.

Thinking to turn and run away from the haunted past, Old John froze in his footsteps with the next scream. "Sa fini jamais!" He exclaimed. (It never ends!) Then, absently running his fingers through his unkempt, thinning hair, he turned and walked down the dark hallway.

He slowly turned the handle on the door and peered inside. A kerosene lantern burned low in the corner of the room, barely giving off enough light to see. Nis lay atop the ruffled bed in a tight ball. From somewhere deep inside him, John felt compassion. Something he had not felt in a long time. Nothing deserved to suffer that badly, he thought as he approached to loom over her.

Flashbacks of the war still threatened to make him want to run, yet he fought them, remembering once, that amongst the fury of a bloody battle being fought for possession of a small village, he had stopped, hearing a woman's cry and helped with the birth of her child. John was surprised at himself for remembering the incident. He was a hard, callous man. And yet he remembered the feeling of awe as he had held the newborn infant in his hands. Life, amongst so much death.

Another scream tore from Nis setting John into motion. Through tear-ladened lashes, she watched as her uncle began moving around the room. Then he was over her, straightening her legs, murmuring something to her. Oblivious to anything but the searing pain coursing through her young body, she did not struggle.

A dream. She must be having a dream. Floating in and out of consciousness her mind struggled to comprehend the sound of a baby crying. All she could be sure of at the moment, however, was that the pain had ceased. Opening her eyes, she watched as her uncle bent over at the foot of the bed. Then he raised up and walked over to her side placing a small bundle in the crook of her arm. He turned to gather the soiled linens he had used then quietly walked out the door, closing it soundlessly.

A beautiful, clear sky greeted John as he stepped off the porch. He turned his head ever so slightly, picking up the sound of a baby's cry. As he made his way to the back of the house, he feverently hoped the Treater had explained how to feed the child! He tossed the blood-soaked linen into the barrel used to burn their garbage, then lit a match.

Fire and blood always seem to go together, he thought to himself, watching the flames consume the cloth.

The days turned into weeks. The weeks into months. Nis, being a child herself, reveled in her boy child as she watched him grow with each passing day. The love she felt for her babe was something indescribable. It was all-consuming, but the most wonderful feeling Nis had ever known. She was no longer lonely.

Though Uncle John had been there at her time of need he still walked around her as if she was not there. He had always been that way. Not cruel, just not demonstrative of any emotion. After the babe was born, Nis saw him even less than before. She had even tried to prepare special dishes for him, to, in a small way, thank him for his help. But the meals were never touched. She would have never believed him capable of helping her for anything, but he had and she would never forget.

It was a particularly beautiful day. Nis finished her chores excitedly, watching her babe as she did so, and wanting to be outside to enjoy the beautiful, early afternoon.

She loved to watch her child play. Her love for him encompassed her. Squeals of delight would emerge from her as she watched the babe attempt to walk, only to fall down, unharmed. She was totally unaware of being the focus of someone's attention as she continued with her favorite pastime.

Stan was mesmerized by the sight in front of him. Well hidden from sight, he crouched down in the thicket of brush.

He had returned home for a break at school three days earlier, and could no longer resist the urge to ride out and see for himself, if what he had heard was true. The whole town was talking about it, Stan's sister Dee, had informed him. "That Ol' Uncle John did it to his own niece! And she had a baby for him. Yuk!"

Dee was two years younger than Stan and, as usual, her endless gossip and chatter caused Stan to walk away from her. God but she was shallow! Though he loved her as his only sister, he could never remember liking her.

It had been the evening of the graduation that Stan had found out the girl had lived. He knew he would always remember those torturous days of expecting, at any moment, to be arrested, or questioned for the crime of murder. Even though Sly and Fred had assured him constantly that there was nothing to worry about. "The girl was nothing but 'white trash,'" Fred had interjected in the conversation. "Even if the authorities could prove we were there at the time, nothing would be said or done about it. Each of us know our parent's standings in this hick town." Fred asserted.

Sly and Fred had jokingly teased Stan about his nervousness. To Stan, they seemed to not care about what had happened. But the memory of the girl's face still haunted him.

The relief he felt when Fred had told him that his father, Ned Long, had ridden out to Old Uncle John's the day of their graduation to purchase some "corn water" to celebrate his only son's graduation and commented on seeing the girl. "It's a shame she's 'daft'," Ned Long had commented, sadly.

"You saw her, Pop?" Fred asked, his heartbeat quickening.

"Sure did." Ned Long replied as he lifted a box onto the counter. "But, of course, as she was walking into the woods. Ol' John does not like her to be around when anyone comes over. Always sends her away. She is a pretty thing though. Never did know the story of her parent's death and as how Ol' John ended up with her care."

Fred had not replied. Had his father been looking for any changes in his son's behavior he would not have seen any. Fred, being from such a small town, knew his family's hardware business was a strong leg to the town and without the Long Hardware Store people would have to drive as far as Baton Rouge just to buy a hammer. Yes, Fred felt, he had clout in the town and he did not mind bragging about it. As far as the 'white trash' girl of Ol' Uncle John's was concerned, he could care less. Besides, he never got a go at her anyway! Stan had been the only one to have a taste of that!

As Nis reached down to lift her babe, the sun twinkled off the small, braided, gold chain on her wrist.

Absently, Stan rubbed his left wrist remembering that he had lost it the night of the attack. He had searched his mind trying to remember where he could have misplaced it only to come to the realization that he must have lost it in the struggle with the girl. And now, as his stomach threatened to lose the breakfast from that morning, he knew.

People say the girl's "not right" he thought to himself as he watched her playing with the child. But to look at her and listen to her musical laughter, Stan thought the people might be wrong.

The simple cotton dress that hung loosely on her body, belied the shapely form that it concealed. Hair, dark as a raven's wing, and long from having never known a pair of scissors, reflected deep colors as the sun bounced off of it.

Stan was even more transfixed as she turned her flawless, oval shaped face in the direction of his hiding place. To him there was no way to describe her eyes. Almost void of color. Blue? His mind questioned. No. Though they could be considered a blue, he knew not to have ever seen such a color. Or lack of it.

Why had she kept the bracelet? He wondered. Did she know it belonged to him? Why would she keep anything to remind her of that night?

The questions rolling over in his mind could only be answered by what, only a few moments ago, he had dispelled. The girl was surely "daft". Nothing else made sense.

Quietly, Stan sank back into the woods. One question still ate at him. The one question he had come quietly, without telling anyone where he was headed, to find out. Was the child his?

Emerging from the woods and back on the dirt road, another question arose. "Did it matter?"

Chapter Three

HOLLYWOOD, CALIFORNIA

"Quiet!...Annnnnd Action!" came the director's cue from behind the dimly lit scene.

"Shhhh, my darling." The woman cooed as she held a very young child in her arms. "Daddy will return home soon. We must be brave for him." Tears welled up in the woman's eyes, providing visual evidence of the heartfelt pain of her words for the camera.

"Cut!" The director all but screamed. "For God's sake, can't we do anything about those eyes? How in the hell are we supposed to make something seem real,...believable...If we can't believe it ourselves!?" Running his hands through his thinning hair, he looked down at the floor, then looked up and screamed, "The woman looks blind! She has no eyes!"

With a sigh, Anna released the beautiful seven year old child actor she had been holding. The youngster had fit so comfortably in her arms. As for the tears needed to play this role, they came easily enough. So easy, in fact, that the only roles she could get anymore were those the critics liked to call "tear-jerkers".

Anna smiled at her young co-worker and new friend, as she stood up, absently straightening out the long, dark, tightly-fit dress she had been instructed to wear for the part of a suddenly...supposedly...widowed woman.

In a matter of seconds, Felix was at her side. "Anna, I'm sorry. I..."

Anna put up her delicate hand to stop him from saying anything else, "It's all right, Felix. Just set the matter straight. I'll be in my dressing room." With that, she primly walked off the set.

Felix watched her as she retreated. Her walk, as always, was as elegant as that of a queen. It had been his lucky day the day she entered his office, presenting a letter of referral from one of Felix's closet friends. Stunningly gorgeous, had been his first thought as he took in her face and graceful appearance. But could she act?

That question was short lived as he gave her her first screening that very afternoon.

"Excuse me, sir," he called to the frustrated director, before going into his well-rehearsed spiel about his client's unusual eyes.

Once in her private, yet temporary dressing room, Anna sat down. She felt exhausted. Though she was certainly grateful for this leading role, she knew all too well that she needed a vacation. For so many years she had buried herself in her work. Neither her friends nor colleagues, had been able to convince her of the fact that she was pushing herself too hard, too fast.

Not even her brother, Leone. She smiled to herself recalling the many times he and she had almost come to the point of screaming at each other over what they each thought was best for her. She knew he meant well and only had her interests in mind, yet she knew she had to do this. Acting had always held her interest.

As a small child she would dress up to imitate some actress she had seen or met at one of her parent's socials. Then, as a young woman she had finally been able to convince her father that it was the only thing in life she wanted. Still, though, he had hoped that it was just a phase of her young, spirited mind. Perhaps she would soon tire of it all and become acclimated to the position into which she was born. She was a countess after all.

Anna excelled in her acting capabilities, an excellent student at her craft. Her passionate desire, and her beautiful voice soon separated her from the other students. She had no time for friendship and cared for none either. Her family was all she had ever needed, for they loved her dotingly. They never ceased to shower her with affection.

Leone, in particular. Though he was her senior by fully a dozen years, she had always loved and adored him. His strikingly dark, good looks only added to his calm, gentle demeanor. He was, she knew even at a very early age, quite a catch for any girl.

Anna awoke at the sound of Felix's urgent voice calling her, as his powerful fist pounded on the door. Dismayed, she realized she had fallen asleep in her chair, her head resting heavily on the delicate, white vanity table. "Coming," she answered, hurriedly checking her make-up and straightening out her dark gown. As she exited the small dressing chamber, she was still a little confused as to what possibly had taken her back in her memories of her family.

Perhaps Leone was planning a visit to see her. She could almost feel his presence at times, and then he would show up. That must be it. Many years separated their births but their hearts were as one.

The chauffer-driven sedan pulled up to the double, wrought iron gates that provided entry to a secluded nest of small, but luxurious townhouses. Anna waited patiently for the driver to open the door at the stoop of 20 Olivette Terrace. True, she was considered a celebrity by all standards, and by now, accustomed to such behavior from the chauffeur. Then again, she had always been treated in this fashion.

She was born into the luxury of having someone see that her every whim was fulfilled. People who did not truly know her might think her stardom had gone to her head, carrying herself in such a queenly manner as she did. However, this was the only life she had ever known.

Tess, her maid, was gone, Anna noted as she entered the foyer. As was Tess's usual routine, Anna knew there would be a meal prepared for her and that her night clothes would be laid out neatly on the antique settee in her dressing lounge.

The apartment was small by comparison to what Anna had always been accustomed while growing up, and even smaller compared to the home she and Seth had bought not long after they had been married.

"Seth," she said aloud as she absently took off her long gloves. Lord it had been ten years since his death, and she still missed him!

Pouring herself a small glass of Drambui, Anna took a sip, savoring the thick, sweet taste of it. With a sigh, she turned to walk up the stairs to her chambers.

After filling her ornate, oval-sized tub, she stepped into the refreshing warmth of the water gratefully and gracefully sliding into the milky, white bubbles.

"Ahhhh," she moaned, feeling the warmth of the water invade and soothe her weary muscles. It had been a long day. Thinking back, Anna recalled falling asleep earlier in the day. Her brows furrowed. She could not recall ever having done such a thing. Perhaps it was a sign of aging. A small smile tugged at the corners of her mouth, remembering when she thought forty was ancient.

Then, closing her eyes, Anna let her mind drift, wistfully, back to the happy days of her youth. Those were the days when she and Seth were so deliriously in love. They had been drawn to each other from the beginning.

Anna had come home after a long but fulfilling six months of performing in a smash Broadway production. She had not been given the lead, as she had hoped. Instead, the producer thought her quiet, soft demeanor and strong voice, better fit the character needed to support the leading lady. Anna, not one to bicker, had quietly accepted her role. She knew in her heart that one day she would outshine them all—those she considered would-be actors. It was not by any means a malicious thought. It was just something she knew.

Anna had the cab stop a block from her parents home. She wanted to surprise them. Looking at the plush onyx dial of her petit Bulova wrist watch, she smiled knowing they would just be sitting down for tea in the parlor, as was their usual custom. Her parents had not had the chance to come see the play, so it was with great zeal that Anna burst through the door, warbling the refrain from the musicals' best known tune.

Newton DeLeiu jumped up from his seated position. Elegantly dressed, a slight blush to his face, he stared at his daughter, acting so blatantly.

Lady Ann, Anna's mother, at first startled by the intrusion, now looked down at her folded hands. It was a struggle for her to fight the mirth threatening to be unleashed in an unbridled applause. She was, after all, a lady and they did have a guest.

Anna, quite caught up in her role of singing and pirouetting across the richly glossed mahogany floor, had not noticed the tall man now standing beside her father.

With all the elegance of a swan, Anna curtsied into a low bow, as the butler came into the room, totally confused. Head down, Anna waited for her performance to be recognized. Then it came. A loud, boisterous laugh. One she did not recognize. Her face shot up. Anna, now red-faces, stood taking in the view before her. Her eyes widened at what she had done. She had been so excited about coming home, it had not occurred to her there might be someone else there.

"Ahumm," her father cleared his throat. "Monsieur Bradford, may I introduce my daughter? Lady Anna De'Leiu.?"

"How do you do?" Seth had asked, walking over to a still, red-faced Anna and placing a soft kiss on her hand.

"Monsieur," she acknowledged, pulling her hand free and noting the laughter dancing in his deep blue, mesmerizing eyes. "I am afraid I must apologize for my behavior..." Anna stumbled.

"No, please," he said, holding up a large, muscular hand in protest. "I assure you it was quite entertaining!"

Anna was quick to note the genuine laughter in his voice and could not help herself from smiling back at the tall, handsome, man before her.

Seth was totally entranced with the woman. She was very petite, with long, raven colored hair. Her small, oval shaped face, still slightly flushed from her embarrassment, was flawless. But it was her eyes that seemed to grasp him. Almost void of color. Like the lightest blue one could imagine without almost thinking them white. Her eyes were such a contrast to her dark hair and olive skin.

"Yes, well," Newton Deleiu, interrupted. "Daughter, it is wonderful to see you. I trust everything is well with you?"

"Yes, Papa," she assured her father as her mother entered. "Mama, I have missed you so." Anna approached primly and kissed her lovingly on the cheek.

Lady Ann smiled and returned her daughter's affection. Then, turning to the gentlemen, she said: "If you will be so kind as to excuse us, I will see Anna to her chambers."

Both men nodded, and watched as the women retreated from the room. Halfway up the enormous, winding stairway, Anna could not resist the urge to glance back at the handsome visitor standing so erect in the doorway of the parlor. Her eyes locked with his and both smiled at each other. "I like him," she thought to herself, knowing that in just a few more minutes, she would have all the information she needed about Monsieur Bradford. That is, if her mother knew anything at all about him!

After that night, Anna and Seth were rarely apart. Anna had questioned her MaMa until her mother threatened to call PaPa up just to be able to satisfy her excited, beautiful daughter, about the young man.

Meanwhile, downstairs, It was all Seth could do to keep his mind and conversation on the topic he had come to discuss, which was information about the true French culture he needed so desperately to finish his second novel.

Anna was startle back to the present. Her bath water had grown tepid, but she hardly took notice as she realized someone was downstairs, buzzing her at the gate. Reaching for the large, plush white towel, she quickly wrapped herself. Water cascaded down her slim, shapely legs as she answered the upstairs intercom.

"Yes?" she inquired somewhat nervously. It was highly unusual for anyone to be calling on her at this hour.

"Bon jour, Mademoiselle Anna!"

"Leone," she squealed, excited to hear his voice. "I will unlock the gate. Please come in and pour yourself something refreshing to drink. I shall be down in a flash!"

"Oui." Came his soft, reply. Then, answering the slight buzzing of the electric gate, he pushed through the wrought iron and entered. He paused briefly to hear it click and lock back in place behind him.

Leone entered the immaculate apartment. Looking around, he surmised that nothing had changed since his last visit. It made him sad. Though he called his sister frequently, he seldom had the chance to visit. And over the years each time he visited her, Leone fervently prayed for a change in Anna's life.

Easing up to the small bar, Leone reached for the dark green bottle of Remy Marten and filled his cordial glass. He thought how lonely his dear sister must be while his life was so full. He had his business, his beautiful wife Lisa, and his two children. He almost felt guilty for having so much, while sweet Anna had no one. If only the baby had survived, he thought for the millionth time. Then, at least, with Seth's sudden heart attack she would have had something. Someone.

A deep feeling of remorse fell over him as he stood staring out the window, unseeing, toward the waves crashing over the wide shoreline of the white-sand beach. How thrilled he had been for Anna as she blossomed with her unborn child. She was happy with Seth, he knew, but with the expected birth of her child she had become radiant!

Then, on the night of the baby's birth, he had gotten Seth's call. "Anna wants you to be here with her, if you can, Leone. I'm sorry about the short notice, but even the best doctors in California cannot stop a Bradford Deleui child from entering this world if it sets its mind to do so."

Leone remembered Seth's voice cracking with nervousness, as he spoke, even though Seth was trying to appear calm. But, despite his best efforts, Leone had not been able to get there until the following day.

Still elated, however, thinking Anna surely to be over the birth of the baby by now, he burst into the room he had been directed to by a sour-faced nurse.

"Darling!" he exclaimed, rushing to his sister's bedside and kissing her on the check before placing the colorful spray of flowers on her lap. Then, from behind his back, Leone produced a snow white stuffed bear. "Didn't want to take a chance on pink or blue," he blubbered, noting the look of sadness spread across her face.

"What has happened?" he asked, knowing it was serious by the look an Anna's face and watching as Seth left her bedside to go and stare out the window.

"The baby," she winced, struggling with the words, "Our baby is missing."

Leone felt an unfamiliar coldness rush through his body. "Missing?" Leone exclaimed as he quickly turned his attention to Seth at the window. "I don't understand. How could this happen?"

Slowly, Seth turned and walked back over to his wife's bedside. Without looking at Leone he said: "We are not sure ourselves just what has happened. We have been questioned all morning by detectives. They seem to think our baby was taken by a nurse working here."

At that moment, a short, portly nurse entered carrying a small tray. "If you gentlemen will excuse us, the doctor has ordered a sedative for Mrs. Bradford."

Leone watched as Seth placed a kiss on Anna's cheek. Still unable to comprehend the situation, Leone followed Seth through the door of the private room.

In a nearby waiting room, Seth explained the events of the last 24 hours as best he could. The suspect nurse had been hired only recently. "She was the last person seen in the nursery and had disappeared along with the infant shortly after 1 a.m. The local police feel that the name she had given on her application is not her real name. They have assured us that they are doing all they can to find out.

"The police feel that the child was taken, possibly to be ransomed back to us," Seth had ended.

But that never happened. The long hours turned into days, then months. Anna became more and more withdrawn and despondent.

Anna had been released from the hospital the next morning with the assurance from the local authorities that everything was being done to find the baby. The physician, Dr. Nolan McConnell, had told Seth that he felt Anna might recuperate faster by being surrounded by her family at home.

Lady Ann, their mother, had greeted them when Anna returned home days after the birth and with empty arms.

Leone remembered his mother's swollen eyes. He knew she had been crying over her daughter's loss, but being the strong woman she was, she never let on once Anna had returned to her home. Lady Anna took full charge of running the household.

Time offered no relief for the once happy family as chimes from the tall grandfather clock in the foyer rang incessantly each hour after agonizing hour without interruption. Days, weeks and months were lost to all family involved as their worst fears came alive.

No contact from the abductors. No ransom request.

Leone was brought back to the moment by his sister's soft voice. "I should have known you were coming to visit!" Anna announced as she descended the stairs.

"Oh?" Leone responded inquisitively, smiling broadly. He was glad to have been pulled back from the painful memories of the past. "Am I to believe your psyche once again informed you of my coming?" he jested.

"Oui, Mon Cheri" she answered, kissing him lovingly on the check. "I have always seemed to having a sixth sense where you are concerned."

"True," he admitted. "So, how are you?"

"Oh, I am fine, as always."

Anna tried to appear cheerful, but Leone noticed the dark circles under her eyes. "You look tired. Is Felix working you to death?"

Pouring herself a small drink of her own she sat on the cushiony sofa, "Please, Leone. I'll not argue with you tonight. Truth is I am a bit tired. I was thinking about a long vacation. Perhaps I will return to Paris for a stay."

Leone stared at her for a moment. "Are you ill? Is something wrong?"

She laughed. "Nothing is wrong and I am not ill."

"But you have never…You always…"

"Disagree with you about what is good for me." She finished for him. "Oui, I am truly guilty of that. Perhaps it is because I am starting to get older that I am learning to appreciate life a little more. PaPa has always tried to instill the impression in me that life is precious. One should enjoy life's gifts and not rush hurriedly through them." With a sad sigh she looked to Leone, "Perhaps I am finally able to grasp his concept."

The trip back home for Leone was troublesome. Try as he might he could not ever remember seeing his sister so unemotional. So lifeless.

He paid no heed to the taxi as it sped through the busy, congested street to take him to his destination. Absently, he pulled a bill from his pocket handing it to the driver then stepped out onto the platform of the airport.

"Thanks!" the driver yelled, then drove away, pushing the hundred dollar bill deep into his pocket.

After settling in his seat on the aircraft, Leone ordered himself a strong drink. God, why had life cheated Anna so? He hurt for her. And for the millionth time, Leone silently wished he had been able, through the years, to bring her some closure regarding the loss of her baby. Any news about the child would have helped. Even, he thought sadly, to know the child had died.

◆ ◆ ◆

Stan Peterson walked quietly across the polished, mahogany floor then hesitated at the huge, double oak doors leading to his father's study. He was well aware of what awaited him on the other side and did not relish the thought.

"Enter," came the reply to Stan's hesitant knock.

"Father? You wished to see me?" he asked, hoping his demeanor belied the nervousness.

Franklin Peterson sat at his large desk, studying the papers before him. "Yes, Stanley. Please sit down." He motioned with his hand toward the leather Queen Anne chair facing him.

After a few moments, Franklin retrieved one of the papers he had been studying on his desk, then cleared his throat. "It seems that the dean at Yale is not satisfied with your achievements. He is curious to know if you are the same person who had far surpassed their standard evaluation exam. He thinks there has been a mix-up of some sort regarding one Stanley Peterson."

With that said, Franklin Peterson put down the sheet of paper and looked into his only son's eyes. "We seem to have a problem."

Stan squirmed under his father's glare. Try as he might, he could find no way to explain. He knew he had not kept up with the criteria of the position he had sought at Yale. He knew, full well, the amount of money his father was lavishing on his education and not to forget the generous contributions to the prestigious school of political science.

"I...I am sorry Father. I cannot explain it." He all but whined. Then, before he could stop himself, he blubbered, "It is just that...that there is so much going on. I confess to getting caught up in the excitement. The parties. The girls. It is a different world there." He lied. For if anything, he had become a social outcast. Not the least bit interested in participating with any of the activities regarding the school.

Franklin watched and listened as his son rambled on and became even more furious than when he had first received the letter. He stood and pounded his fist on the desk. "Enough!" He screamed loudly. Then, taking in a deep breath to calm himself, the 45-year-old father said, firmly: "Need I remind you that you are a Peterson? My Father saw to it that I was accepted into Yale and I was damn proud of it! I worked hard to keep my grades at a level of acceptance. That world was as different to me as what you are belly-aching about now! Even more so for me! A potato farmer's son for Christ's sake!" He shouted.

Then in an even louder, harsher tone: "You are, at least, accustomed to fine clothes and the elite of society! Pray tell what area are you having trouble acclimating yourself to?!"

Stan was ready to bolt from the room. He knew the temper of his father and knew by now even the servants were aware of his heated, not so private, father-son discussion. Slowly, on trembling knees, he rose from the chair, "I will do better," he mumbled. Barely audible.

"Better?!" Franklin screamed, unable to control his disgust.

Just then the double doors opened.

Both father and son turned to face the demure woman standing in the doorway.

"Mr. Peterson," she said, sternly addressing her husband. Then she turned to her son, her tone softening ever so slightly. "Stanley." She entered the room after closing the double doors behind her. "I was out in the rose garden and could not help but hear the meeting taking place in here. I gather," she turned to her husband, "there is a problem."

Franklin Peterson looked at his wife of 23 years. An extremely thin woman, with few distinguishing features that time had neither enhanced nor detracted. Janie Peterson was plain and had been since the first time Franklin had ever laid eyes on her.

Her family had been fairly well-to-do, and though at times, throughout the years, he sometimes wished he had let his heart rule him—Instead of his ever hungry greed. He could not deny the fact that she had been a large stepping stone for him. That is, her money and status had smoothed the way for attaining his ambitious goals.

Still, he could not deny the fact that she was kind. Janie loved her husband and showered their two children with affection. Too much, he thought, at times. As was the case now. He knew without a doubt she had come to his study to protect her precious son from his overbearing harangue.

"Now P.J.," He addressed her by her nickname. It was a name her father had attached to her as a small child. It was with love and affection that she was called P.J. The name meant Plain Jane. "You need not come in here to try and undermine the seriousness of this matter. You do not know what this is about. Stan does not need your molly-coddling. He is a grown man now and certainly capable of acting like one."

Janie Peterson noted the anguish on her husband's red face. She too, knew his temper, but had learned over the years, ways to approach him in this aggravated state. "You are right, Franklin. I do not know what is going on, but only because you have chosen not to enlighten me on the subject. Perhaps I would not have been aware of a problem if the shutters on the house had not started to tremble from the loud voice in here."

Franklin knew it was too late to exclude her now. He leaned over his desk. Picking up the piece of stationary, he handed it to her. "So be it!" Maybe you

30

can scratch the surface of this son of ours and find the man in him! It is beyond me!" With that said, he stormed out. Slamming the heavy, oak doors in his wake.

Janie looked into her son's soft brown eyes. Her heart hurt for him. His face was pale, she noted, as she motioned for him to sit back down. He did and she scanned the letter in her hands. Looking up, she let out a sigh and asked. "What is the matter? My dear Stan, you have always held up your grades. Quite easily, I might add."

Stan said nothing. Listening to his Father's tirade was one thing, but his mother's gentle coaxing was even more formidable.

"You were so excited about college," she prodded. "This was something you have dreamed about for years. What has changed your mind?" Her voice was soft. Filled with true compassion.

Stan struggled with himself. The truth of the matter was he was not sure himself. Everything he had ever aspired for was laid out before him, yet none of it interested him anymore. Nothing seemed to drive him. His mind did not have far to search back to find when things had gone awry. The hard part was wondering why he had been unable to put it behind him. Like Fred and Sly had.

But, to his gentle, loving mother he said: "It is just a phase, Mother. I do not mean to cause you and Father grief. I have been neglectful of my responsibilities and promise to change."

Janie looked into her son's eyes and saw the unhappiness in them. Something was very wrong. But what? When? Who? And why?

Sherry Jo Saunders

◆ ◆ ◆

The bell clanged loudly over the door as Ned Long
looked over his shoulder. He was stocking batteries on
the higher shelves and was not able to get a clear view
of the customer. "Be with you in a moment," he
yelled. He finished the task then wiped his hands on
his apron. "Mr. Peterson! Good to see you. How
have you been?"

His greeting was genuine and Franklin took the
offered hand to shake. "Well, Thank you," he
responded.

"What can I do for you today, Sir?" Ned asked,
trying to recall if Franklin Peterson had ever been in
his store.

"Well, I was wondering if that boy of your's was
around?"

"Is something wrong?" Ned asked anxiously.

"No, no." Franklin assured him. "I, um, just
wanted to ask him something." When Ned made no
move to answer, Franklin continued. "It's about
Stanley. I know he and your Fred are fairly good
friends and I just…"

Ned held up a hand to silence him. "I understand,
Sir. I'll go get him for you. He's in the back. Just
please let me know if he's done anything. Although he
is an only child, I'll not have him doin' wrong."

A few moments passed before Fred entered the rear
door, following on the heels of his father, who held a
firm grip on his shirt collar. "Mr. Peterson? My Dad
said you wanted to speak to me?"

Franklin studied the young man before him. Chubby would be the word to best describe him. And a bit too cocky, for someone of his low status, he thought. Though the young man had, on occasion, been over to visit his son Stan, he always appeared to be out of place. At least to Franklin's way of thinking.

However, Franklin Peterson kept these thoughts to himself and asked: "Do you think you could take a little time off and take a ride with me?"

Fred looked to his father, receiving a curious nod, and said, "Sure.'

"We will not be long, Sir," Franklin assured a concerned, Ned Long.

Peterson's driver opened the door to allow the two men inside, then silently pulled away from the curb.

Fred noted that Mr. Peterson had not given the driver instructions so he assumed their destination had already been discussed.

The sedan they rode in was, to say the least, luxurious. Fred, unaccustomed to such richness, felt quite comfortable as he stretched his legs out in front. Someday, he thought to himself, running his hand over the soft, cool, leather, I will live like this. Not like the old man. His dad was too conservative. Well, maybe stingy was the better word.

"Could I offer you a glass of cool water?" Franklin Peterson asked.

"Yes, please," was Fred's polite response.

Franklin pulled down a small door between the seat behind the driver exposing different sized lead crystal glasses and a sliver pitcher. Fred noted the different decanters on the shelf and knew they contained alcohol. After pouring two glasses Franklin offered Fred a drink.

"Er…excuse me for being so blunt, young man, but you do not seem to be concerned as to why I have asked you to talk with me."

Fred took a sip of his water. "Well, sir, I figure it must be about Stan."

Franklin's eyebrows furrowed. "Yes. It is. I'm impressed with your astuteness," He lied.

"Well, what else could it be sir?" Fred asked, a confident smile on his too-round face.

"Well," Franklin said, sitting back in his seat more comfortably. "Now that we understand our subject matter, I was wondering if you could help me." Franklin felt that if he handled this young man correctly he might be able to find some answers regarding his son's strange behavior of late.

"If I can help in any way, I will do so," Fred answered too eagerly for Franklin's taste.

"Good. Good." He leaned forward toward Fred and said: "I'm not sure if you have noticed it or not, but something is terribly wrong with Stan." He allowed his words to sink in as he studied the younger man's face. Was that a smile he saw flicker, briefly?

Franklin continued: "Stan seems so…so, well, depressed. His grades at school have plummeted. His mother and I are very worried about him. So, I thought that you, being a friend of his, might be able to help shine a little light on the matter for us."

"I see, sir. And yes, I noticed Stan's behavior when he was home last week. But Stan, and I mean you no disrespect sir when I say this, he is awfully tender-hearted at times." Fred confided.

"Would you elaborate on that a little for me?" Franklin asked, not sure of where the conversation was headed.

"Well, you know, Sir. Sometimes us guys, well we like to cut up. Have some fun. And Stan, well he takes everything much too seriously."

"Ah. I see." Franklin said. Then said, understandingly. "You guys are just wanting to sew some wild oats in other words. Well, I can certainly understand that. After all, I was once a young man much like you."

"Yes, Sir." Fred smiled, easily. He was not sure if Mr. Peterson knew anything about that night in the bayou or not. But he knew at the very least that Stan's father sensed something. And Fred was not worried one bit about what had happened that night. After all, they were just out having fun. They did not hurt anybody. As far as that Ol' Uncle John's niece, well she was just trash anyway. Who cared?

"Do you think you might know what is troubling Stan?" Then came the extra encouragement he felt needed, as he withdrew a bundle of bills from the inside of his dress coat pocket. "His mother and I would be very, very grateful."

Fred watched as Mr. Peterson began to count out the money. All the bills were in hundreds and Fred felt his mouth go dry. "I would be very happy to help you out, Sir."

Franklin took the young man back to his father's store and thanked him for his help. He instructed the driver to head toward home, then poured himself a generous glass of scotch.

So, his son had been a party to a rape. According to that fat weasel, as he now thought of Fred, Stan had been the only one to have had a chance at the girl.

The young man had been right in his saying that Stan was too tender-hearted. If this was what was troubling his son, and he was almost positive it was, then he would help Stan get through it. He did not condone this behavior, but damned if he was going to let some little piece of bayou trash ruin his son! They would deal with it. And one thing was certain. P.J. must never find out!

◆ ◆ ◆

Two weeks from the day Franklin Peterson had visited with Fred Long, news came to shatter his life.

The Peterson mansion sat back from the small lane. The red-bricked circle drive allowed visitors entrance to the massive double, oak front doors of the white, two storied building The lawns were immaculate as were the 40 acres that surrounded the large home.

Franklin was sitting on the oversized sofa, a small glass of sherry in his hand. He was listening to his wife as she played a gentle melody on the polished, black Steinway piano. He loved to listen to her play.

They each heard as the bell rang announcing a visitor, yet neither moved. They knew Jack, their butler would answer.

A moment passed before the middle-aged man-servant entered the room. "Excuse me Sir. There is someone at the door who wishes to speak to you."

"Who is it?" Franklin asked, irritated that his quiet moment was being interrupted.

"It is the sheriff. He says it is very important."

"Aw, very well." He rose, wondering what Arthur Jacobs had come all this way about. After all there was a telephone at his disposal.

"Please come in, Arthur," he greeted the stocky man. Noting the taut expression on the man's face, he asked, "Shall we step into my study?"

"No. Frank. I just…Well, Sir, It's about Stan." The sheriff squared his shoulders and said, "He's dead, Frank. The police in Lafayette parish just notified me. I came on out as fast as I could."

The small glass of sherry Franklin held in his hand slipped, shattering onto the polished floor. He heard Jack gasp then heard a strange animal sound behind him. He turned to see Janie crumble to the floor. The animal cry had been hers.

He watched, stunned, as the sheriff and the butler hurried to her side. Stan? Dead? It could not be true! There was some sort of mistake! There has to be!

◆ ◆ ◆

The funeral for young Stanley Peterson was an event the town would talk about for many years to come. The small flower shop in Cypress could barely keep up with the orders for memorial sprays. The day before the funeral the owner, Jim McConnell, had hired three people to assist him working all through the night to fill the orders. The money he had made had been worth it. Making more in three days then he had in the last two years.

The Petersons were a powerful and wealthy family. It showed in the staggering number of

37

acknowledgments of sympathy from friends and business associates.

The memorial was closed-casket. It was said the body was unrecognizable, having been burned so badly that dental records were used for identification. Though there were those who believed it to be an accident, with young Stan going over the cliff in his car like he did, the police reports read as suicide. There had been no tire marks on the road to show an attempt to brake the roadster. The alcohol in his blood indicated that Stan was highly intoxicated.

Though the family tried to dissuade the rumors and claim another vehicle had run their son off the road, there were many who believed it was suicide. But why? People asked.

Janie K. Peterson sat, unmoving, on the hard, wooden pew of St. Mary's Catholic Church listening to the parish bishop as he praised her son's noble qualities.

"Stanley Peterson was known to all as a kind young man…" said the bishop.

Franklin glanced sideways at his wife and noted the proud bearing in her shoulders. She was holding up well, he thought, considering she had not been out of her bed since the tragic news had arrived. The family doctor had prescribed some sedatives, which seemed to help her stop screaming Stan's name over and over. He, for the first time in his life, was at a loss as to what to do to bring harmony and order back into their home. Deep down inside he knew things would never be as good as before. Why had he decided to wait until Stan's next visit home to talk to the boy? Why had he not done something as soon as he had found out about his son's troubles? The question would forever haunt him.

He had rehearsed, over and over in his mind, what he would say to Stan. He would show his understanding in his son's shame over the event, but life goes on, he would stress. He would even try to offer the girl or her uncle some type of compensation. If the girl was daft, as Fred Long had claimed, the uncle surely would accept a monetary gift for any trouble his niece had experienced. Besides had he not heard Dee talking one morning about the uncle having his way with her himself? She had said something about the girl having a child.

Franklin no longer heard the quiet, praiseful words being said about his son as his mind began to wonder. A child? Could it possibly be?

Charles McLane turned off the two lane road and drove through the huge wrought iron gates. He noted several workers in the yards and knew it must be a full time job for them to keep the lawn so immaculate. Yes, he admitted to himself, the Peterson home was the most extravagant place around these parts. And out of place, was his thinking.

The butler, as immaculate as everything else around, answered the door.

"Yes, Sir?" Jack inquired.

"Mr. Peterson is expecting me. Charles McLane."

"Yes sir, Mr. McLane. Please step into the sun room. Mr. Peterson will join you in a moment."

Jack took the man's hat and coat then left the room. The sun room was very fittingly described, Charles thought as he walked around. There only two structured walls. The other two sides were glass. On one side you could see the small creek flowing through the property, while the other over-looked a large vineyard.

"Charles!" Franklin Peterson exclaimed as he entered the room. "I am very glad you came to see me on such short notice. Please have a seat and allow me to get you a sherry."

"Thank you," Charles said. He watched as Franklin poured two small glasses. There were dark circles under the man's eyes and Charles knew he was still grieving over the loss of his only son. He had not seen Franklin since the funeral. That had been a month ago.

"Here we are," Franklin said, handing Charles the glass. "Not too early in the day for you I hope."

"Never too early for a good glass of sherry," Charles said with a broad smile.

"Yes, well, as I said, thank you for coming."

Charles took a sip. He waited patiently for Franklin to open the discussion, addressing the urgency of the meeting.

He did not have to wait long.

"The reason I asked you over is to discuss a delicate subject. I could not think of anyone else who might be able to help. That is, help with discretion."

"Discretion?" Charles asked.

"Yes. You see, well, let me start by asking you if your son Sly has talked to you about Stan."

Charles put his glass down on the polished table beside him. He was not sure where this conversation was headed. "What about Sly and Stan?"

"I gather you don't know," Franklin acknowledge, solemnly.

"Know what, Franklin? Maybe it would be best if you just got to the point." He was trying to remain calm, but Franklin seemed to know something about Sly. Though his was not the closest relationship ever between father and son, he and Sly had always been able to communicate well with each other, or so he had always believed. What was it Franklin was trying to say?

"Our sons," Franklin choked, and Charles saw the mist come over the distraught man's eyes. "You see there was this young girl…"

Charles barely moved as Franklin reconstructed the night as best he was able from all of his inquiries. The graduation ceremony the boys had with Ol' Uncle John's corn water. The girl. The rape.

A part of Charles was relieved to know his son had not actually raped the girl and yet another part of him realized that, as he thought to console his grieving son over a friend's death, his son had held back information into Stan's death. It was a lot for him to swallow.

"I had no knowledge of this occurring," Charles commented, sadly. "I never believed Stan committed suicide. Sly agreed with me that it had been an accident."

"Yes, well," Franklin said, clearing his throat loudly. "Stan inherited more of his mother's genes than mine, I am afraid. Too sensitive! I always told her she molly-coddled him too much!"

"So you really believe that Stan was unable to deal with what he had done, to the point of committing suicide? Were you not able to talk to the boy? Make him understand that though it was wrong, it was the whiskey. The excitement!"

"No!" Franklin screamed. "I was not!" He stood, agitated, pouring himself another glass of sherry. "By the time I realized just how depressed he was…It was too late."

Charles let out a deep breath, suddenly feeling drained. He had only moved to the area three years earlier. It had been a profitable move. During those years, he had only seen Franklin Peterson on social occasions. He did not "know" the man, but the did have respect for him as a man, for his hard work and for his status in the community.

As for Stan, Charles had liked the young boy. He knew Sly and Stan were close friends and had welcomed his son's companion into their home.

Charles was jerked back from his thoughts as Franklin voiced: "This is why I called on you to help me."

"What can I do?" Charles was totally confused, yet compelled to ask.

"The girl has a child. A boy." Then to compound Charles' already bewildered state, he said, "I want the child."

"Dear God, man! What are you saying?"

"I believe, well I know the child is Stan's. I have seen him." He lied.

"But you can't be sure!" Charles protested. "And, even if that is the case, you can't take a child from its mother!"

"In this case, I think I can." Suddenly, Franklin was calm, as if all the bad news was over. A gleam came into his eyes and he said: "The fact of the matter is, we need the boy. Think of what we have to offer him! A home! An education! The girl is living in poverty and they...well, people say she's not quite right in the head. And, as for her uncle, everyone knows what he does for a living."

"Still, Franklin, I'm not sure this will be for the best."

"For the love of God, Charles! Think of what it would mean to Jane. She had lost her only son. Think of the good that can come from this. Jane can not have her son back, but she can have a piece of him."

Charles shook his head, still concerned. "Why have you included me in this? What service can I provide you?"

"There are two reasons I need you. One, I want someone, an attorney at law to assist who does not know me. You know a lot of people, so I thought you might be able to refer me to someone. And two, I will need Sly's testimony. He can serve as a witness to that night and a character witness against the girl."

◆ ◆ ◆

"The papers have been drawn up, Mr. Peterson" the attorney explained over the telephone. "I put a private investigator on the case three days ago, and he assures me that things are just as you say. The child is being raised in an environment much below human standards. And the mother of the child does not appear mentally stable."

"Wonderful!" Franklin exclaimed. 'When can we get started with the custody suit?"

"It should not take long. I have already requested a court date. I will have photographs and, of course, our witness if we need him. It should be a cut and dry case. I will let you know when I will be arriving."

"Thank you." Franklin put the receiver back on its hook. Soon, he thought to himself as he started up the stairs to his wife's bedroom. Soon she would be up and back to her normal self. He could not tell her what he was doing quite yet. But it would not be long. His P.J. would come out of this deep depression once she had the child. He just knew it!

He entered Janie's room. Though it was well after noon and a beautiful sunny day, it was hard to detect in her room. The heavy drapes were drawn tight, keeping out the light. The still form on the large, canopy bed, tugged at his heart. She had not been out of this room since returning from the funeral.

The medication she took kept her still and quiet. The doctor had assured him this was normal behavior. One day she would wake up and start trying to live again. After all there was Dee, and their daughter needed her mother.

But as each day passed, Franklin began to realize even more how much his P.J. had adored their son. That was why he was pressing so hard for the child. She needed him.

Quietly, he left the room. There was still a great deal to do.

◆ ◆ ◆

Nis heard the vehicle as it neared the house. She had just put her child down for his midday nap and hated the thought of getting him up. She knew to leave the house out through the back way whenever anyone came to see Uncle John, but she did not have the heart to drag the sleeping child along with her.

He was sleeping so soundly, she thought to just leave him and step out back behind the small shed. After all, most visits from the townfolk were short. They were only there to bargain for the corn water, so it was with little worry that she sat, leaning against the tin shed, listening, waiting for the customer to leave.

It was a clear day. The heat had not yet reached its height and the small breeze, drifting off the swamp, was welcomed by her as she waited patiently for the sound of an engine to start up. The customer certainly was taking their sweet time, she thought, getting anxious. She had a lot of work to do today and had planned on finishing the tub of laundry while her babe slept.

Looking down at her small hands, she touched the newly formed blisters. She had chopped wood the day before until she thought her hands would bleed. Normally the chore was done every other day, but Nis thought to go ahead and have enough cooking wood to last throughout the week.

The more chores she could complete early gave her more time to spend with her child. And it was time that she needed, for he was prone to get into everything. Curious about everything in his little world.

Whether it was a cricket to chase or the hot cooking stove, he wanted to touch and feel everything around him. With the hot stove she had tapped his hand and sternly scolded him with a "Non!", then felt her heart constrict when she saw the tears well up in his soft, brown, eyes. She picked him up, immediately cradling him next to her bosom. It was hard on her to think she might hurt the only thing in the world she loved. But her common sense ruled, telling her it would be harder on her to know her child would be injured from the burn.

Feeling restless and wanting to hurry back to the house, Nis stood, brushing the debris from her backside. If the customer did not leave soon, she would just have to sneak back.

Then, she heard a card door slam. Knowing it was the car that had driven up, she started back toward the house.

Unseen, she peered out the front window as the car drove out of sight. Nis was relieved, feeling she might still have enough time to finish the wash before her child woke.

Two huge tubs awaited her on the back porch and, humming to herself, she attacked the chore.

She hung the last of the cotton squares on the line. Thank goodness Uncle John had thought about diapers. He had come in her room the morning after the baby was born with a bolt of white cotton cloth.

He put the cloth on the scarred dresser, and unrolled a small piece. Then he reached for the hunting knife, always worn on his side, and cut the soft cotton material.

Nis watched intently as he gently put it on the babe's bottom and secured it with a large pin. She knew, though no words were spoken, it was his way of teaching her what to do.

With the chore behind her now, she picked up the straw basket and stepped back into the house. It was time for the child to be waking. Slowly opening the door to the tiny room she shared with him, Nis blinked, not once but two times. Her eyes were not quite adjusted to the dark room after being out in the bright sunshine.

She blinked a third time before realizing the small cot was empty. Even the small blanket she had put over the babe was gone. Panic!

She turned and ran back down the short hallway. Heart beating wildly, she searched every room of the tiny cottage. Under everything he could have crawled. Then, out the front door she dashed, looking left, then right. Nothing. Then the thought of her son wandering into the thick woods, toward the Bogs, set her a frenzy. "Tan!" she screamed over and over. "Tan!" The tree limbs tore at her face as she ran blindly calling out for her child.

She reached the area of the Bogs then willed her feet to slow down. One wrong step and she would be swallowed up. Her only prayer was that somehow the child was with her uncle. It was the only thing that kept her from going mad with worry.

She entered the clearing and could see Uncle John standing by the huge barrel, a fire glowing hot below it. Unaware of the blood and dirt on her face she stumbled toward her only hope.

John turned toward her as she entered the clearing. The tears were flowing from her eyes, mixing with the blood erupting from the cuts on her face. She held out her arms beseechingly and cried...

"Tan!"

John then turned slowly away from her. Nis watched, horrified as he disappeared into the deep swamp. Confusion, mixed with the realization that he walked away from her, caused her to fall to her knees, shaking violently with grief.

"Noooooooon!" she screamed. "Noooooooon"

John halted in his steps as he acknowledged the sad cry. "Sa me fait de la pain," he murmured to no-one. (I am sorry)

Chapter Four

Baton Rouge, the capital of Louisiana, was a bustling town. Noise filled the air from the automobiles as they hurried to and fro. People, seemingly in a rush to reach their destination, paid little heed to the billowing white clouds, contrasted against the bright sky above them.

It was a clean town with wide sidewalks and merchants of every kind imaginable inhabiting the stores lining the sides of the busy streets.

The white, brick courthouse sat alone in the middle of the town. Evenly trimmed shrubs adorned the stone stairway leading up the veranda. Tall, two storied white pillars supported the porch, with large, mahogany doors centering the entrance. A smartly uniformed officer stood by the entryway.

Inside, giant fans rotated ever so slowly from the ceiling helping to stir the air and cool the occupants.

Franklin Peterson sat quite comfortably in a chair beside his attorney. The attorney had not come cheap, but Franklin had been told, straight out, by Charles McLane, that he would be expensive because he was the best. Franklin had wanted the best, as always, and did not hesitate when the attorney had quoted him his price. Now, confident in all that was taking place, he listened as Judge Samuel Oliver, a long-time friend, began speaking to the man representing his case.

"Very well then, you may submit the photographs. And, are you ready to call your first witness?" The judge inquired.

"Yes, your honor," Franklin's attorney replied. "If it pleases the court, I would like to call a Miss Bonnie Calhoon to the stand."

"Very well then," the judge acknowledged.

A woman, middle-aged and overly thin, approached the stand raised her right gloved hand and swore to tell the truth in the matter at hand.

Franklin's attorney opened his examination by asking: "Miss Calhoon are you now and have been for 12 years employed by the state of Louisiana as a child welfare worker?"

The witness answered the question in the affirmative as Franklin glanced at his watch. He had been assured by all parties that this proceeding would not take long. It was merely a formality.

As it turned out, much to Charles' relief, his son Sly, had not needed to testify. Sly's testimony, if not handled correctly, could have proven malice with Stan's actions, whereas now, Franklin did not have to worry over that part of the testimony. Still, he felt that with enough money offered, the boy would have said exactly what he would have been told to say.

As it turned out, after the local social service officials had reported on the child's environment, it would not have mattered at all. That it was his grandchild was assured. The facts were strong enough for him to get custody of the child for whatever reason. As long as a more suitable environment was provided.

"Very well then, you may step down," the judge said to Miss Calhoon before turning to the defense.

Then, to be bespectacled defense attorney, he asked: "Do you have any witnesses you wish to call on behalf of this case Mr. Knowlin?"

"Ah, yes, your Honor," Knowlin all but whispered. He shuffled the papers n front of him and said, nervously; "If the court will bear with me a moment."

"Am I to understand your witness is not in the courtroom?" The judge asked clearly agitated.

"Ah, yes your honor, that is correct," he said, nervously pushing the dark, rimmed glasses up on his nose. "You see, sir, my witness is the child's mother and she had to be heavily sedated in order to bring her here. However, I have just been informed that she is awake."

"Mr. Knowlin! Must I remind you of how valuable the court's time is? If you have a witness in this case, I advise you to bring them forth now or forfeit the chance."

"Yes, your honor. I believe that is her now. Then, your honor, I call to the stand, Miss Nis Fern."

A uniformed officer of the court entered the room. On his arm was a very slim, young girl. She had her arms wrapped tightly around the heavy-set man's bent arm for support, as he all but carried her down the aisle and to the witness stand.

Franklin's attorney stood. Pity filled his heart as he took in the tattered blue dress, at least two sized too large, and the dark, long, unkempt mass of hair that now covered the young girl's face. His stomach began to feel queasy watching as the bailiff continued supporting the girl now being sworn in.

His view was obstructed by the bailiff, who was now asking her to raise her right hand. She was just as he had been told, a child herself. The queasiness in his stomach grew.

He had taken on this case as a favor for a dear friend, Charles McLane, and it had seemed to be a logical case of a grandfather fighting for the rights of his grandchild. Especially once he, himself, had gotten all the facts. And the pictures! To think someone could survive in such a seedy dwelling as portrayed in the investigator's photographs. As well as the report he now held in his hand, that read: "No electricity, no sanitary toilet, no running water.' It was one thing for the mother of the child to bear such a life, but for the sake of the innocent child, it was intolerable!

"Do you understand?" the bailiff asked the girl again. When the woman-child remained mute, Judge Oliver intervened.

"That will be all, Lucas," he addressed the bailiff, dismissing him. Then, to the state attorney, he said: "Mr. Knowlin. It appears that your witness is not capable of understanding the events taking place here today."

Franklin Peterson put a hand over his mouth to hide his smile. He had told Knowlin that it would be a waste of time to produce the girl. He had expressed the fact that the girl was "not right". But the stupid little man insisted that she be given the right to defend her motherhood. What a joke!

Turning to share his mirth with his council, he watched, concerned, as his attorney turned the strangest shade of white. The papers in the man's large hands slipping quietly to the floor.

Leone Deleiu, a very much respected and sought-after attorney, had watched as the bailiff was dismissed, therefore clearing his view of the young witness. This was the moment he needed to close the case. He stood and raised his face to address the judge. "You Honor."

Suddenly, the girl looked up, pushing the heavy, dark, hair from her face with her small, trembling, hands.

At that very moment, Leone saw her. He felt the papers slip from his hands and felt powerless to do anything about it. The room began to spin and it took every ounce of willpower he possessed, to pull his eyes away from the beautiful, delicate, young face, as she continued to try and bring her heavy, dark mass of hair, into some sort of semblance. But it was not the face alone that so startled him. It was the girl's eyes.

Stunned, Leone stared at Nis. As if suddenly hypnotized and frozen. Though his body remained motionless, Leone's heart did not, for he knew whose eyes he now looked into. Anna's eyes. His mother's eyes. His grandmother's eyes. Then, barely audible to anyone, he said: "Nis." Swallowing the huge lump that had formed in his throat, he continued, louder: Annissa." He closed his eyes. "Oh, my God!" He cried, placing his hands over his face.

The murmur in the courtroom graduated from a low rumble into loud voices as the judge gaveled out obedience for silence.

Nis shivered from all the confusion and drew back, shrinking into the back of the leather chair. She was terrified and it showed as her eyes grew large. The uniformed officer had all but run back to the frightened child, standing in front of her protectively.

It was then that Leone took a deep breath and pulled his jumbled thoughts together. Everyone was watching his strange behavior, waiting...

"Counselor?" the judge spoke sharply. "I am not sure what is taking place here. Perhaps you would care to enlighten us all!"

"Your honor.," Leone stammered. "I beg your forgiveness. It is just that...that." He looked back at the terrified girl, noticing the officer patting her hand. His eyes locked with hers. Tears welled up and choked the words momentarily. Then: "I cannot possibly represent Mr. Peterson in this case. With all due respect, your honor, I know this young lady. I believe it would be a conflict of interest."

Chaos ensued. A few local reporters had come to the courthouse after learning that Franklin Peterson, the famous, rich real estate tycoon, was involved in some sort of custody suit. They now felt like this story could escalate into something big and began shouting questions from the pews.

"In my chambers, gentlemen!" Leone heard the judge scream out as he, ignoring the melee surrounding him, slowly walked over to Nis, who now tried to retreat back behind her uniformed, protector. The man eyed Leone, suspiciously.

"It is all right," he assured the bailiff. Then, reaching out his trembling hand, he gently, lovingly, touched her cheek. "Mon Cheri. You have brought the sunlight back into my eyes."

Nis saw the tears glistening in the tall, handsome man's face. She did not understand his words, but somehow she felt him to be a tender, gentle man. Perhaps he could help her get her child back. Pleading eyes met his. "Tan?"

Franklin Peterson was hysterical. Watching the tender scene being played out before him, he screamed: "You son of a bitch! I will have you disbarred for this!"

With Franklin's outburst came a flash of bulbs exploding as the photographers were quick to get a picture of the angry, red-faced man standing, pointing his finger and screaming profanities.

"Please take her into the waiting area," Leone instructed the bailiff. "I have to meet with the Judge." Then, with Franklin's screams resounding throughout the building, Leone added: "Do not let anyone near her."

Leone entered the masculine office of Judge Oliver. Mr. Kenneth Knowlin, the appointed public defender in this case was already seated, nervously, rifling through some papers on his lap. Judge Oliver had taken off the heavy, black robe and sat at his large, ornately carved desk. His chin rested on a tightly clinched fist.

"I apologize to your court, sir," Leone said. "These are extenuating circumstances of which I am sure you will understand, when you learn of them."

"For you sake, counselor, you had better be right."

Meanwhile, Nis sat, absently toying with the gold bracelet on her wrist, on a hard chair in the cool hallway. The large, uniformed, man seemed to be protecting her as he refused to budge from her side. Once, a man had hurriedly come down the hall and her newly-found protector, positioned himself in front of her. The man passed by giving them both a quizzical glance.

She wished she could understand what was happening. Nis, after all, had been able to understand little of the words that were being spoken. Her own vocabulary supported few English words because there was never anyone to share them with in conversation. She never had been taught. Her Cajun dialect was taught to her by her uncle and other than occasionally having the Treater come by, Nis spoke to no one.

One thing she felt was certain. This was all about Tan. Her son. She concluded that the man, Peterson, had taken Tan. But why?

Nis tried not to think about that night. The memories were too painful. They, the three of them, had hurt her, badly. They had bruised her and the one she thought the most beautiful had hurt her most of all. She cringed at the memory. Though she managed to block most of the event out of her mind, all she had to do was look into her precious son's face and she would again see her attacker.

Sometime later, as Nis sat, she heard the clicking of shoes on the polished marble floor. Her head rested in her hands and she did not look up until she realized the shoes had stopped in front of her. Raising her face she was once again looking into the kind eyes of the man who had touched her face.

Leone thought his heart was going to burst. He could not escape the resemblance. She looked so much like her mother. There was no denying this was Anna's, his loving sister's, child. She was the mirror image.

He sat down beside her. "I am not sure if you can understand me. I do not believe you to be daft, as you have been portrayed." Anger rolled in his stomach at what he had almost been forced to do. Forced, in the sense that the information given to him had been incomplete!

Making himself calm, so as not to frighten Nis anymore, he said, softly: "I have attained temporary custody of you and you will be staying with me for a few days." His eyes misted again and he said: "There...There is someone very special, who desperately will want to see you."

Nis had cocked her head trying to read the man's expressions. Why was he so sad?

Leone stood and held out his hand to her. Gingerly, she placed her very small, hand in his, then watched again as his eyes swell with unshed tears as he turned her hand over, gently rubbing the blister in her palm.

◆ ◆ ◆

Leone and Nis took the taxi the few blocks to the Le Mark Hotel. Glances at her, told him she was frightened. He wished he could make her understand what was happening but she barely spoke. And the times she had tried, he had not understood her words.

Watching her face as they entered the luxurious hotel, he was once again stunned by her beauty. So like her mother's. How could anyone have thought this child belonged to that old man? Even in the too large dress she wore, her appearance was striking. Her hair almost touched the floor, having never been cut. And despite her ragged look, she was very clean.

Her skin was smooth with an olive hue. A complexion inherited from their ancestors. And though Leone, probably might have been able to recognize her as a relative, the eyes left not doubt. As far back as the family was able to trace, all of the females bore the same colorless eyes. A trait his family was very proud of.

Many questions ran through his mind about just how she had come to be in Louisiana in the first place. Questions that would be answered. He would see to that. But for now, he would take care of the business at hand first. He would put his family back together. Then he would see some justice. He relished the thought.

Now, how to tell Anna?

◆ ◆ ◆

"Hello? Anna?"

"Oui Leone. It is good to hear from you. How have you been?"

"Fine. Just Fine. Listen, cheri, I was thinking about a visit to see you."

"That would be wonderful! When should I expect you?"

"Tomorrow, if that is not too short a notice for you."

"Not at all. I would love to have you, Lisa and the children. It has been such a while since Lisa and I have talked."

"Well…"

"Is something the matter, Leone? You sound a bit tired."

"There you go with your psychic abilities again." He joked. "Actually, Lisa and the children are not with me. I have just finished a case in Louisiana and I am too close to pass you by." He lied.

Anna laughed. "You are just feeling a bit of guilt, Leone. Do you realize it has almost been a year since we last saw each other?"

"Time flies, mon cheri." As soon as he made the glib remark, he wished he were able to take it back. Time had not flown for the sister he loved so dearly.

They each said good-bye and Anna quickly dialed the number of her salon.

She had not been well for the past week. ' Her lack of appetite clearly showed in her weight loss. And hopefully, she prayed, her stylist could help in hiding the dark circles under her eyes. It would not do to have Leone see her looking so gaunt. He would rant and rave!

After setting the appointment, Anna called Felix, her manager, and explained that she would need to leave rehearsal a little early tomorrow as Leone was coming for a visit.

"Good. You need the rest," he chimed back at her.

Anna put the receiver back on its hook. Rest? That was what she did not want. The nightmares had been so horrifying as of late. She dreaded sleep. Perhaps this visit with Leone would help.

After Leone's brief conversation with Anna he rang for the hotel manager. He had very little time to prepare for his visit with Anna and, after a few moments, the manager assured him he would be able to help.

The oh-so proper concierge, in his tuxedo, was probably curious about Leone's request for clothes for a young lady, but four small words— "Money is no object" —silenced him.

Leone's next call was to Felix, Anna's long-time friend and manager. He felt he could trust Felix. Anna certainly did. Leone had always felt Felix had more of an interest in his sister than she realized. A very distinguished gentleman, Felix catered to Anna's every whim. She seemed to be the only one who did not notice how his eyes lit up whenever she was near.

Leone sensed she had suffered too much loss in her young life to ever hope for happiness again. First, her newborn child, then her husband. She tried very hard not to show her feelings, but Leone knew.

A quick conversation with Felix, asking for a moment of his time on the morrow and Leone was back to the business at hand, Annissa.

The suite he had rented at the hotel was as luxurious as he had ever see. Leone was quite used to such accommodations and always sought out the best hotels whenever he traveled. He had left Annissa in the large sitting room and chose to make the calls from the bedroom. Now, as he entered the sitting room, he found her staring out the window.

Arms locked securely over her breasts, Nis had not noticed his entry. Leone took a moment to study her. He knew she was frightened. He could not even begin to know the things she had been forced to endure in her young life. Could not even imagine.

Had she been beaten? The question made him want to take her and hold her as he would Sher, his own daughter. Sher was two years Annissa's senior, yet he still thought of her as his baby girl. Leone, though, knew it would probably terrify the child even more for him to touch her now.

That brought to mind the question of Stan Peterson. During his investigation, Leone had been led to believe the young lady had been a willing partner, a girlfriend. He had believed the young girl had willingly had sex with Franklin's son. Now, as once again the anger threatened to spill forth, clinching his fist tightly, he thought not. She was a child. Fifteen, he knew. He had been there at the hospital after her birth. He would remember that day until he died. That meant she had only been fourteen when the incident occurred. Had she been raped? Anger that someone so special to his family might have suffered at another's hands reinforced his need to find out. Someone would pay. And it would not matter the cost.

Even if he were not a fairly famous and most sought after attorney, and Anna a very famous singer and movie star, Leone's family, the DeLeuis were very well known. And very wealthy. Psychologically, he drew strength from his family's history. There would be an answer to all of this, he vowed.

A knock at the door allowed Leone a brief respite from the ugly thoughts. A young woman, with a very friendly attitude, strode through the doorway. She introduced herself as the owner of the small boutique in the hotel lobby.

With professional accuracy, she measured a bewildered Annissa, oohing and aahhhing over the pretty girl's hair. Annissa kept shooting quizzical glances at Leone. He just smiled, hoping to convey that everything was all right. The lady left, after assuring Mr. DeLeui there would be a selection of outfits, with accessories, before the day was out.

Leone ordered dinner for two to be delivered to the room, feeling Annissa would not be accustomed to eating with strangers. The sumptuous meal consisted of everything from shrimp cocktail to filet mignon. Fresh baked bread with melted butter. A large garden salad with freshly cut vegetables.

Leone pulled the plush, upholstered dining chair out for her and she sat. She just stared at what lay before her. Never in her whole life had she seen so much food. It was almost too beautiful to touch, let alone consume! "Pooyah ee! She exclaimed with delight. She waited to see what the nice man with the kind eyes did and tried to mimic him as best she could. She was starved.

Leone hid a smile. Noticing that she did everything exactly as he. Pride. He mused. She had pride personified. Then, still thinking of her strange outburst, he thought to try to understand some of her strange language.

Lifting one of the large shrimp from the small, decorative glass, he said, "Shrimp."

Annissa, in turn, did the same, saying: "Cheuvrette."

Leone smiled. For though her accent on the word was strange, it was French. Holding up the dinner fork, he said, "Fork."

Annissa found the one she believed to be the same size, as there were so many of them, and held her's up, saying, "Fourchette."

Leone again smiled and without saying anything this time, held up the silver salt and pepper shakers. He raised his dark, thick eyebrows, waiting, but

Annissa only shrugged. She had no idea what he was now holding, but they were so lovely!

"Salt and pepper," Leone said. Annissa continued to stare at him blankly. Leone then poured a little salt on the linen table cloth, followed by the pepper.

"Ouai," She exclaimed, childlike. "Sel et pimet!"

Leone was thrilled to watch her beautiful, young face transform as she appeared to be a little more at ease. They each continued to eat in silence, but somehow a bond was now forming and Leone was content. Time would break the language barrier and he pictured Annissa, very astute, unlike what the other's had said, becoming the countess she was destined to become. A title bestowed upon her by his family long before she was even conceived. It was her inheritance.

◆ ◆ ◆

That same afternoon, as Leone was preparing to put the missing pieces of his sister's life back together, there was another at work whose sole purpose was to keep it torn apart.

"Sign it Sam!" Franklin Peterson ordered.

Judge Samuel Oliver looked back at his long-time friend and was well on his own way to losing his temper. "Dear God Frank! I cannot just put my signature on this document!"

"Why not? You have the authority! You know what this means to me, Sam."

"Yes, Frank, I do. But I also have a responsibility to Louisiana state law. I cannot just change a legal document."

"There is nothing to change. The child's birth has never been recorded. There is no birth certificate showing that he even exists!" Franklin all but screamed. "This is a blank certificate. I have already filled in the information making Janie and me his legal parents. All you have to do is verify the document."

"What you are asking me to do is illegal, Frank. I do want to help you but…"

"By heavens, man! My wife is dying! I need this child. It is the only way I can think of to possibly bring life back to her. You will do it, Sam. Or you will never sit on another bench." He leaned over the judge's desk, menacingly close. "You and I have spent quite a few evenings together, my friend. Do not think, for a moment, I would not tell of some of our most memorable moments at Lady Seymour's"

Samuel was taken aback by the onslaught. He had never seen Frank behave in this manner. Yet, he knew the man was unscrupulous when it came to something he wanted badly. Samuel was quick to remember Franklin's boasts of how he had once quarantined a piece of land he wanted, after the discovery of oil on the property, therefore sending a mother with four small children out to fend for themselves. The man had no conscious. Black gold was becoming more and more prevalent in Louisiana and Franklin sought to own as much property as possible. "Easy money," he had boisterously exclaimed.

With a heavy heart, Samuel Oliver reached for the small piece of paper Franklin had thrown on his desk. He signed it, then had his secretary come in and witness it.

Franklin snatched the paper, barely allowing the ink to dry. He waited until the secretary had left the room and said: "This was only a formality, Sam. You did not have to make it so difficult. The child will be better off with us. You know that. What could that white-trash girl offer Stan's son?"

Samuel felt exhausted. Franklin had entered his chambers in such a huff that he had not even given him a chance to explain a little of what exactly had happened today in the courtroom. Now, he said: "For all or our sakes, Frank, you had better pray that what I learned today is not true."

Franklin had his hand on the brass handle of the door ready to leave. With a smirk, he asked: "And just what was that?"

Sam looked his friend square in the eyes and said: "That little girl, you keep referring to as 'white trash', might possibly turn out to be the missing child of Anna Bradford."

"The movie star, Anna Bradford?" he asked, incredulously.

"The very same," Sam offered, tiredly. Then, he listened to Frank's laughter as he slammed the door behind him. The loud, obnoxious laughter continued on down the corridor.

◆ ◆ ◆

"There is a Mister DeLeiu to see you, sir."

"Thank you. Bea. Please ask him in."

"I did ask him into the foyer, sir. He said he would prefer to wait for you at the door."

Felix frowned. He had been expected Leone. The man called last night requesting to see him first thing in the morning. Why did he not want to enter the house? "I will see to it, Bea. Thank you." His maid retreated and Felix went to greet his mysteriously acting guest. "Leone!" Felix extended his hand in a friendly gesture. "It is good to see you. It has been a while."

"Yes, it has," Leone returned smilingly.

"I have already figured out what it is you have come to see me about." Felix stated.

"Oh?" Leone asked.

"Yes, and I must tell you in my own defense, of course, that I have tried and tried to explain to that sister of yours how important it is that she take a vacation. Get some rest! So, save your chastising for her, pardon my language, stubborn little ears!"

Leone smiled. He could well imagine what Felix went through to make a point with Anna. Stubborn was a very choice description. "Ah, yes, Felix. I agree with you. However, that is not exactly the reason I came."

Now it was Felix's turn to ask, "Oh?"

Leone reached behind him to produce a young girl. Felix had not noticed her behind Leone. "Felix, I would like to introduce to you, Annissa."

Felix more confused now, took in the appearance of the girl standing before him. She stared at the floor, apparently too timid to lift her face. Her hair was as black as any he had ever seen and incredibly long! It had been carefully braided and draped over her small, left shoulder. Even braided, it hung down past her knees. She wore tan silk slacks, a matching long-sleeved blouse and slippers, on her feet. Felix looked to Leone, questioningly.

"Annissa," Leone spoke to the young girl, softly. "May I introduce you to Felix Chalmers."

Then, with Leone's prodding, Annissa looked up into the stranger's face. "My, God!" Felix exclaimed. "Do you have any idea who she looks like?" He was asking, not able to take his eyes off the lovely face. "Those eyes! I have never known anyone to have that color...except Anna."

Leone noticed the color draining from Felix's face. "I apologize for not coming in. I did not want to just thrust her on you and you on her." Felix had no conception of Leone's prattling and it was clearly written on his features. "Well then," Leone attempted, "I feel I could stand for some coffee."

"Coffee?" Felix responded, still trying to untangle his thoughts. Then. "Oh. Yes. Please excuse my lack of manners. Please come in. Please."

Felix led them into his spacious living room. Then, quickly stepped out to place the order with Bea. "Well, then," he said, coming back into the room where his visitors awaited him. "We shall have coffee momentarily," he said as he watched Annissa moved about the room, touching the different items as if they were foreign to her. "Who is she?" He finally asked, uneasily, trying to understand why the girl's presence unnerved him with her familiarly stunning beauty. "A double, looking for a job?" Lord knows, he thought to himself, she certainly would make a perfect double for Anna. Although she would need special makeup to help with the age.

"Forever an agent huh, Felix?" an amused Leone offered.

"Then enlighten me, Leone. For I am truly amazed at the resemblance!"

Bea then entered to place the coffee urn and porcelain cups on the table beside the over-stuffed, white sofa. "I will pour the coffee, Bea. Thank you." Felix said, dismissing her.

Leone assured Felix that the young lady did not care for coffee and Felix handed Leone the fragile imported china cup with matching saucer now filled with the steaming, hot brew. Felix, realizing that Leone had as yet not answered his question, said: "Well?" He gingerly took a sip of his coffee and leaned against a small bar, studying Annissa.

At that moment, Leone blurted: "She is Anna's daughter, Felix."

Felix took a hard gulp, feeling the hot liquid sear his throat and cut off his airway. Desperately, he tried not to choke; to just keep the liquid down until his breathing became normal again. It was to no avail. The thick liquid escaped his lips, spattering coffee all over the small bar that held the snifters and the cross-cut leaded crystal decanters.

Leone jumped up and began slapping Felix furiously on the back. Even he had taken the shock better than Felix, Leone thought. Then, just as quickly, he pushed that criticism away. After all, he had almost fainted when he looked into that face! If they, being the strong men they were supposed to be, could not handle the news very well, how in hell was Anna going to react?

Chaos seemed to be the rule, for just as Leone was helping Felix to finally draw a deep breath without more strangulation, there was a loud crash in the foyer. It was then Leone noticed that Annissa had slipped quietly out of the room. Alarmed at the thought of her being harmed while in his care, and after so many years of not knowing what had happened, he raced to the entryway, leaving Felix to his own care.

The scene he met as he dashed into the foyer stopped him in his tracks. The maid, Bea, had also heard the commotion and came running. Leone stopped her by raising his hand and motioning for her silence. After a few seconds, he whispered to Bea to go check on Felix. "He was choking," he said, not taking note of the alarm in the woman's face as she dashed off in the direction of her boss.

The oil portrait of Anna hung majestically over a small stand positioned in the center of the hall. It had been painted a decade earlier, as Leone recalled. Felix prized it above any of the masterpieces or items of fine art he had acquired.

The vase that had been holding a fresh array of flowers on the stand below the portrait now lay in a thousand pieces. Water stood in puddles on the marble floor.

Leone watched, mesmerized, as Annissa climbed onto the cane-back chair sitting by the flower stand, then reached her small hand out to touch the face of the woman in the painting. Annissa noticed him from the corner of her eye, and jerked back.

"Nis," she said. Then she pointed to herself and back at the portrait. "Nis."

His heart went out to her. Without fighting the urge any longer he went to her and gently put his arms around her. She did not back away, but he took note of her lack of response.

Felix, now breathing a little easier, entered the hallway and took in the tender scene before him. At first, he took no notice of the shards of Chinese pottery or the damp flowers scattered about the floor. Felix saw only Leone as he held Annissa, tenderly. Then, realizing they stood in front of the portrait of Anna, he surmised it to be the reason for the melee. Noticing that Bea now stood beside him, he said softly: "We can clean this mess later."

Leone pulled away from his beautiful niece. "That person in the painting, Little One, Is your mother. Your MaMa."

Nis had no recollection of the word, MaMa. So Leone's attempt to make her understand was useless. He knew as soon as the word slipped from his mouth, for she showed no sign of comprehension.

"Could it be, Leone, that she is deaf?" Felix inquired as he, too, noted the absence of understanding with the child.

Leone had not realized Felix's presence until he spoke. "Would that it be that simple, Felix. It seems to be more a language barrier. I was told she was raised by an old man deep in the swamps of Louisiana. Everyone assumed he was her uncle. The language spoken there is a Cajun dialect. It has a French history of sorts, yet I can barely understand it myself."

"That makes it hard to communicate with her, then," Felix acknowledged, before adding; "Leone,

Anna is expecting you this afternoon. What are you going to do? How can you…?"

"That is why I came to see you," Leone interrupted. "I will need your help when I go to see her. This is going to be quite a shock."

"Indeed!" Felix exhaled. "I had always believed the child to be dead."

"Oui," Leone said, slipping back to his native tongue. "I believe it was always easier for us, Anna especially, to believe her to be dead. It was an easier way to deal with such a loss."

"Do you have all the details? How was it that you came about finding her?"

"Perhaps your housekeeper could walk Annissa through your gardens while we speak," Leone suggested. "It is quite a story. One, however, that is far from being over."

◆ ◆ ◆

Anna busied herself awaiting Leone's arrival. She adjusted the silver candelabra for the third time and once more scanned the dining room table. Tess had set places for two. Then, once again, she strolled over to the heavy, gold-framed mirror hanging on the wall to check her appearance.

Her hair had been arranged in a French coif, with two long strands falling gently at the temples. The makeover of her face had done wonders to hide the gaunt look she had noticed in the last week. 'Thank goodness for make-up!' she thought to herself.

Once again, trying to busy herself, Anna checked the imported Chablis, now chilling in the sterling silver ice bucket.   She fought not to remember her nightmares from the night before.   It was hard, for sometimes they would linger, hauntingly, throughout the day.   At times, she recognized them for what they were and was able to tell herself it was from spending too much time along.   Too much time thinking about her life, her family.   Her losses.   But lately, the reveries seemed to revolve around her brother, Leone.   This visit would help ease her mind and heart, she tried to convince herself.   Then came the chime at the door.

Moving to the intercom, she pressed it and inquired: "Yes?"

"It is me, Anna," Leone responded into the small speaker attached to the gate.   He listened as she buzzed open the lock, then entered.   The bricked walkway to her door was lined with small, low-lying shrubs on either side.   Roses of many colors and breed adorned the tiny fenced courtyard.   Leone had always wondered why Anna chose to live in such a small apartment.   It certainly was not the lifestyle of which she was accustomed.   And it certainly was not spacious enough for his taste.   But, then, he thought: "I have a family.   We need the space.   Anna has no need for such extravagances."

Anna literally ran into Leone's arms.   "Whoa, baby sister!"   he chuckled as her momentum forced him to retreat a couple of steps.   "I am getting much too old to be swinging you around!"

"It is just so good to see you," she said with a wide smile.   It was that same childlike smile of hers that always managed to get her out of any mischief.   It had always been his Papa's undoing, as well as Leone's.   "How are you?"   She asked, taking his arm and

72

guiding him into her comfortable parlor. "And Lisa and the children?"

"Everyone is fine. Bob is enjoying his second year of study in law and Sher thinks the world will end before she can graduate high school!" Leone offered, trying to appear light-hearted.

"Something is amiss?" Anna said sharply, taking note of the sadness in her brother's eyes despite his best efforts to act otherwise. "Let us open the wine and sit. Then you can tell me what it is that has suddenly caused you to look so tired," she stated matter-of-factly. "I hope you are hungry. Tess has prepared a wonderful shrimp casserole for us."

Leone shook his head in wonder. "I had not known I looked so tired. Thank you for being so flattering."

After opening the wine and pouring two glasses, she motioned for Leone to join her on the sofa. He did, taking note of the white leather couch and matching settee, picturing Annissa's reaction when she entered the room. She would touch the material in wonderment, just as she did everything new around her.

"Well," Anna said, interrupting his vision. "If Lisa and the children are fine, as you say, then it must be the case in Louisiana you are working on that seems to be bothering you."

"You are very good with assumptions, you know, mon cheri. Perhaps you missed your calling." Leone jested, somewhat relieved that she had been the one to open the door to the conversation. He leaned forward to place his glass on the small coffee table facing the sofa. "It is, indeed, a most unusual case." he began, hesitantly.

"Please, tell me about it for I do so loving to hear you talk about your adventures."

"Do you remember Charles McLane?" he asked.

"Yes, I do. The two of you were best friends at Yale." She watched him, seriously now, as his struggling became more apparent.

"Yes, well, he lives in Louisiana now. He's making a fast living with his ship-building business. He called a few weeks past and asked if I would do him a favor by handling a local case. It involves an acquaintance of his who is fighting for custody of his grandson."

Ann frowned. "This does not sound like anything in which you would involve yourself."

Leone stood, unable to sit any longer. "No, normally I handle industrial affairs. It was only because Charles requested my help that I agreed. The supposed grandfather is the well-known real estate tycoon, Franklin Peterson."

Anna let out a soft whistle of amazement. She did not know the man, but one would have been from another planet not to know of Peterson's reputation. "Go on," she encouraged.

"Well, the first thing I did, of course, was to inquire about the child's family. I needed information regarding how the child was being raised and to find out for myself why Peterson was so convinced that taking the child away from his mother was necessary."

"Where is the father of the child?" she asked. "Should he not be the one wanting custody instead of the grandfather?"

"He is dead. He was Peterson's only son and the mother is taking it all very badly, I am afraid."

"Yes," Anna barely whispered. "I can sympathize with her."

Leone noted her sadness. This was very painful for him, too, and he wanted so badly to just thrust Annissa into her mother's arms and move ahead to the "happier ever after" part of this story. But he knew all of this would have to be explained.

The more Anna understood, the better able she would be to deal with the problems that lay ahead of them. Leone would need Anna's strength to help Annissa get her son back. Anna had lost her child because of something he did not quite yet understand. And he vowed that never again would anyone steal from his family. Certainly there was no way in hell that Franklin Peterson would take Anna's grandchild!

"I sent at investigator to the area to discover what he could. As it turned out, Franklin Peterson's request seemed to be for the good. The mother and child..." he felt himself starting to choke and reached for a sip of wine.

Anna was starting to feel a little uneasy. Why had Leone's hand trembled so violently when he reached for his glass? Something very serious was happening here, but what?

Leone took a deep breath and continued. "The mother and child were living with an old man, believed to be her uncle. The home was nothing more than a dilapidated shack located deep in the swamp. The uncle makes a living by distilling and selling moonshine. Corn water, the locals call it. There is no electricity. No running water. It is a miracle in itself that anyone could inhabit such a place."

"So, you took the case believing it was in the child's best interest. Believing he would have a better life with the well-to-do grandfather. It is a shame that the grandfather did not think to include the child's mother. She could have benefited from his concern as well."

Leone smiled. What she said was true. "Oui, mon cher. But, the grandfather only wants the boy. The local people believe the child's mother is deranged in some way."

"If that is the case, then how was it Peterson's son became involved with her?" Anna asked, reminding Leone of just how sharp is sister could be.

"I have not found the answer to that question. But I certainly will!" he said vehemently.

"Leone. Tell me why this is troubling you so."

Leone stood and glanced at his watch. Where had the time gone? Felix was to give him an hour to try to prepare Anna. Now, looking at the time, he knew that at any moment there would be a buzz from the gate announcing their arrival.

Annissa had not wanted him to leave her. It had taken quite a while to make her understand everything would be fine. Felix was a stranger to her and Leone saw the fright emblazoned on her face as he left her standing in the arched doorway.

"Leone?"

Leone sat back down, sinking hard into the soft leather cushion. He paused, then took his sister's delicate hand in his. "Anna. The mother is a very young child herself. She is only fifteen years of age. I do not, however, believer her to be deranged in anyway. She is as normal as either of us. I believe she behaves the way she does because of the way in which she has lived. I just could not go through with the case and asked to be relieved from my duty as Franklin Peterson attorney."

Anna's stomach tightened for reasons she did not immediately understand as Leone continued to hold tightly to her hand. Then, she asked: "Why, Leone?"

"The girl was brought to the courtroom. The state attorney believed she had every right to fight against Peterson for her child. It was said that it was necessary to sedate her to bring her so far from her home in the swamp. It was then I saw her." His grip tightened, almost crushing the blood from her tiny, delicate fingers. Yet, Anna barely noticed as the words spilled forth from his lips. "It is Annissa."

"Aaann...?" Anna tried to repeat the name. Tried to comprehend what her beloved brother was saying to her.

Leone thought his heart was going to burst. Tears welled up in his eyes as he looked deep into hers. "Annissa. Your daughter."

"Noooooooo!" she howled, jumping from the sofa and snatching her hand from his as if he had burned her. Her eyes were wide with disbelief. Anna kept staring at him as she backed away, violently shaking her head in protest.

"Anna, stop this! You need to listen to me!" Leone was trying to be forceful. He needed her to be strong. Walking over to her, he held her by her trembling shoulders. He shook her almost forcefully. "Stop this! She is here Anna! She needs you! She needs her mother!"

Leone's words, reaching a fevered pitch, were slowly cutting through the turmoil threatening to overcome Anna. Leone could see that she was on the verge of fainting. He understood that feeling well having experienced a similar shock only hours earlier. He also knew, however, that his sister had strength. More strength than he possessed. He felt he could not have survived the tragedies that had befallen Anna.

"She is here, Anna. She needs you," he said again, this time much softer as he noticed her breathing starting to calm.

Anna pulled away, shaken almost beyond endurance. "She...she is here?" Then: "My child? My daughter is alive? She is here? Are you certain?"

Leone nodded. He felt exhausted. Running his hand through his dark, graying hair, he said: "Felix will be arriving at any moment. I...I wanted to bring her home once I realized who she was."

Anna nodded, still uncertain exactly what was taking place. Then, she once again sat down, thinking about the story Leone had shared with her. "How did she...who is this Uncle? Is he the one who stole her from me?" Anna's tone suddenly began to harden.

Leone had to be strong, but it was very difficult looking into the beautiful, teary eyes of his sister. 'I do not have all the details yet. I did not want to leave her there in Baton Rouge. Not to go back to a life that is certainly not hers. She is grieving horribly for her son. She does not understand what is happening to her."

"You said..." Anna struggled to remember Leone's words. "You said people thought of her as...deranged, I believe that was the word you used."

She seemed to be starting to understand what was happening and Leone breathed a sigh of relief. Never did he want to cause her pain. Once all of this was in the open, they would all benefit from it, he was sure. But especially his sister, whom he loved so dearly and was so alone in this world.

"The language spoken in that area is known as Cajun. Somewhere distantly related to our own French language. She does not speak or understand things being said to her."

"How...Is she all right? Has she been...?" Anna was not sure exactly what she wanted to ask.

"Other than being brought up in an impoverished lifestyle, lacking any knowledge of the world as we know it, she is in good health."

"How was it, Leone, that you came to recognize her?" She asked shakily.

He actually smiled brightly at the question. "Because, my little sister, when I first laid eyes upon her I thought I had somehow been taken back in time and was looking into your own mischievous young face again!"

Anna almost smiled. "She looks like me?"

"Oui. So much, in fact, that when I stopped by Felix's to enlist his help, he surmised that I was trying to get her hired as an actress. Your double, I believe, is how he put it.'

"What was her...or rather...is her name?" Anna asked quietly, swallowing a sob.

"Therein lies yet another question to be answered," Leone said. "She is called Nis. this leaves me to believe that the nurse, who later mysteriously disappeared, looked at the birth certificate. Nis would be a shorter version of Annissa."

Anna was reliving that awful day in her mind when the buzzer sounded. Startled from her vision of the past she looked to Leone. Part of her wanted to bolt out of the room—to leave and not face the painful past. Yet another part of her thrilled at the thought of her daughter being alive. Being with her.

Leone watched the different mixed emotions dash across Anna's lovely face. Then smiled as she stood, squaring her shoulders. "Are you ready to introduce my daughter to me?"

Leone embraced her before heading to the door. After releasing the gate, he went to the door. Moments later, Felix, his young charge in tow, walked toward him. Nis spotted Leone's familiar face and ran passed Felix to get to him. Leone smiled, then reflexively, reached out to welcome her into his arms. She had been frightened when he had left her. Leone had hated to make her feel that he was abandoning her. But, he needed the time with Anna. Felix was the closest baby-sitter, if one could call the burly man such a thing.

Anna watched as Nis ran to Leone. She was lovely! Her dark hair had been carefully braided and now looked to come undone as Nis dashed into Leone's arms. And it was so long! Anna noted the affection Leone exhibited for the young girl as he brushed an escaping wisp of hair behind her small ear. "I braided her hair," he said, slightly red-faced, then chuckled to himself remembering the episode back in the hotel room when he had tried to explain how to use the toilet. Anna smiled proudly at her brother. She recalled how Leone had braided her own hair in a time long since passed.

It was then that Leone turned Nis in Anna's direction. Both women froze. Anna was totally taken aback by the resemblance. Mentally she took note of the child's chin. It was Seth's she thought, and almost succumbed to the feeling that she would faint. Quickly, and with everything she could muster, she shook off the feeling and smiled into the girl's curious stare.

Nis gaped at the beautiful woman. Though naïve, she saw much of herself in the woman standing in front of her. Slowly, she realized this was the woman in the portrait. She released her hold on the man she had become quite secure with and stepped toward the lovely woman, drawn by the haunting eyes that resembled her own. Nis was not sure how, but she felt she belonged here. With her.

Anna noticed Annissa creep closer toward her and could not resist the urge to reach out. She enfolded her daughter and with tears now rolling freely down her own, she said: "My daughter. My beautiful daughter. You have come home."

◆ ◆ ◆

Franklin Peterson drove straight home with the newly-signed document resting in his breast pocket. Today, he felt lighter of spirits for the first time since Stan's death. Upon entering his magnificent home, Franklin inquired of his wife from Jack, his butler of many years. "Miz Janie be still abed, Suh," Jack answered in his own distinct southern dialect.

Franklin took the stairs two at a time as Jack watched, his mouth dropping open in surprise. "Must be they is good news afoot," he mumbled to himself as Franklin disappeared through his wife's bedroom door.

The room, as usual, was dark. Oppressively so. Try as he might, Franklin had not been able to pull his P.J. from the deep hole of isolation in which she now dwelt. Not even their daughter, Dee had been able to rouse her to consciousness.

Dee often sat by her mother's bedside and cried. Begging her mother to talk with her. She missed Stan, too, even though she had always fell second in the eyes of both her mother and father when it came to the distribution of parental affection. But now, the total absence of her mother's love was overwhelming. A 17-year-old girl needed her mother's guidance. She missed their shopping together. The weekly visits to the salon. The few things she and her mother shared before Stan had died.

Franklin walked over to the window and pulled back the heavy drapes allowing the rays of bright sunshine to fill the room. Then, he walked over to his wife, who lay motionless on the large canopied bed. "P.J.?" he beseeched. He noticed the small bottle of medication on the nightstand. He quickly took the bottle and slipped it into his pocket. "No more tranquilizers!" he vowed to himself. It did not matter one hoot to him what the doctor had ordered. He knew what his wife needed, and he would see that she had it! Tomorrow!

Everything was arranged. He had gone to the child welfare office directly after leaving Samuel and had all the paperwork cleared for the custody of the child. His answers to any questions about the child's case had simply been answered by showing the document.

Franklin Peterson was considered one of the wealthiest of all the people in the state of Louisiana. No one dared question him too much. The repercussions would be too severe.

As it was with most of the townfolk, "Yes Sir, Mr. Peterson." came the acknowledgment of his status and it was arranged for Franklin to pick up the child the following morning. Newly named, Rand Peterson would be ready.

It was time, now, to tell P.J. Only he realized he would have to wait until she roused from her heavily medicated state. He stood looking down at her ashen face. "Tomorrow, P.J. Our lives can start again tomorrow."

He left her room smiling. Thinking back on the day before, his smile broadened. "Who in the hell had that attorney thought he was up against?" He wondered. The only conclusion he could come up with, regarding DeLeui's actions, was that the man had intended to take the child for himself. What other reason could there be? Or, perhaps, his mind ventured, "Held on to the child to ransom it back to him!" Whatever the reason, it certainly blew up in the attorney's face! Franklin Peterson now held full custody of Stan's son.

In his study, Franklin sat to reflect on the child. No doubt that he was a Peterson. Franklin had known that after receiving the first photos of him. The child's hair was light and his face was so much like Stan's...

Franklin was not sure just when he had come up with the name "Rand." The investigator had informed him that the child was called "Tan." The name Rand, somehow fell in between, Stan and Tan, or so was his reasoning at the time. "Rand Peterson," he said aloud. Smiling again. He had even been able to come up with a date of birth going by what he had learned from Fred long. Though it was not accurate, the date mattered little. He had registered the child as being sixteen months of age.

"Funny," he thought to himself for the first time. He had yet to see the child in person, his mind reminded him, but the photos had shown him as a healthy little boy. Smiling. Clean. "Who would have thought that that white trash of a family in the swamp was capable of taking such good care of the child?"

Walking over to the window overlooking his vineyard stretching as far as the horizon, Franklin silently praised himself for his accomplishments of the last few days. Because of him, his precious P.J. would soon have a reason to go on with her life. She could once again be the loving, compassionate mother she had always been. As for Rand, he would no longer be forced to endure the poverty he had been subjected to in his young life. He would have everything a child could want.

Yes, things were starting to look up. And if anyone should ever try to interfere with his family, there would be hell to pay! Everyone in the Peterson household had suffered enough!

As for the girl, Franklin had never seen her before today. He had never understood why Stan had gotten so involved with what had happened that night. He could not comprehend why the boy had not been able to shrug it off. See it as it was.

Deep in his soul, he blamed the girl. If she had not teased the young man, had not thrown her trashy self around, then nothing would have happened. Everything would be as it was. As it should be.

Franklin felt justified in taking the boy. The girl had taken his son. He would take her's. An eye for an eye, he reconciled.

Chapter Five

Leone and Felix had remained at Anna's for just a few hours before taking their leave. Leone once again found himself at the train station. The last few days of traveling had almost had him fatigued. But, with this trip, he found his heart lighter.

He smiled to himself remembering how he and Felix had just as well not been in the same room with Anna and Annissa. Mother and daughter were so caught up in each other. Anna, trying to break a language barrier and Annissa simply in awe of her surroundings and the beautiful, kind woman doting on her.

Making himself comfortable for the long ride back to Baton Rouge, Leone pulled a small notebook from the breast pocket of his coat. There was a lot to be done and no time to lose. His first stop would be to visit his old friend. He penciled in the name. Charles McLane.

Making other small scribbles on the page, his mind drifted back to his friend and the early days when that friendship was formed. He had come to respect and cherish the honesty and frankness of his college roommate, Charles McLane.

Though Leone was still considered a foreigner in the eyes of many of the young men at Yale, Charles had been different. Inquisitive about everything from different foods, to the language Leone spoke. In no time at all, Charles and Leone were able to speak in a language other's thought of as unnecessary. French. Who wanted it? Who needed it? A waste of time!

Yet a curriculum needed to be met in order to satisfy the facts of these young men having a taste for all of the world's knowledge.

Charles was eager to know everything. His family owned one of the largest tuna fleets and canneries in America. Being the only male heir, he was told by his aging father: "You will go to college. You will learn things. You will prosper, by mind, rather than these calloused hands."

Absently, Leone turned up the palms of his own hands in remembrance. He smiled. Charles was a true friend. An open man. One he trusted and loved. While through the years there had been little contact, he knew he could rely on his best friend for any information regarding the reputation of the well known and highly respected Franklin Peterson.

"And how I am going to need your support now, my friend!" Leone thought as he closed his eyes for a well deserved rest. Franklin Peterson would be a tough opponent. One who would probably stop at nothing to get what he wanted. But if there was a weak link in Franklin's chain, Leone would find it. For all of his family's sake!

The next morning, Leone was awakened by a soft knock at the door announcing fresh towels. He had not given up the suite he had rented for his stay in the capital city. He knew that after finding Annissa and delivering her to Anna, he would be returning.

While showering and getting dressed, Leone thought himself to be the luckiest man alive to have found Lisa, his wife. He had stayed in constant touch with her throughout the ordeal and she had been very supportive. She was so anxious, and had wanted to be there when he brought Annissa to Anna. It was all he could do to convince his lovely wife to stay put. To give Anna time alone with her long, lost daughter. He assured Lisa there would soon be a time to celebrate, but not yet.

Leone hailed a taxi in front of the hotel and, after giving the driver the address, settled back in his seat. "It's gonna cost you, mister," the cab driver had quipped. "Cypress is a good two and a half hours from here."

Leone smiled and said: "Everything in this world costs something. Everyone has a price to pay."

The cab driver looked in his rear view mirror. He gazed at the well dressed, distinguished man and wondered if he was talking to him or himself.

Hours later, the cab drove through the gates where a huge sign hung overhead, proclaiming "McLane Boats". Leone was impressed as he looked around. He paid the cab driver and tipped him well. He would no longer require his services for he knew Charles would be able to supply him with transportation.

The boatyard was noisy with activity. Hammers banged loudly as burly men worked on what looked to be the skeleton of a large trawler. Others busied themselves painting and putting the finishing touches on other vessels.

Charles had always possessed a lust for the sea and a passion for exploring its depths. This was a perfect setting for Leone's dear friend.

A small building erected high up on stilts held a small sign indicating it was the office. It was in that direction Leone headed. Climbing the narrow stairs, he was able to look out over the large yard.

One commercial boat, at least 300 feet long, rested in a cradle. It looked to be completed. A dark-skinned man, shirtless, sat on a scaffold slung from the bow apparently painting the name in large, blue letters.

The day was warming. Leone—dressed as he was in a cotton undershirt, heavily starched white dress shirt snug at the collar, neck tie and vest—felt grateful for the coolness of the small office as he stepped inside. He had taken off his fashionable blue seersucker jacket and carried it draped over his arm. He placed his small attaché case on the floor.

"Can I help you, sir," a young woman, looking to be in her early twenties, asked Leone with a warm smile.

"Good morning," Leone said. "I am here to see Mr. McLane."

"Is he expecting you, sir?" She asked the tall, very handsome man with the distinctive accent.

Leone smiled, showing his even, white teeth and causing the woman to think him even more handsome. "Yes," came his reply. "Though no definite time had been specified."

"Mr. McLane is in the yard, but if you will bear with me, I will have him paged on the intercom." She pressed a button on a small, upright microphone and called for Charles to come to the office. The receptionist then bade Leone to have a seat.

Within moments Charles came bustling through the door. His dress was casual. A short sleeve shirt, wet from perspiration, tan pants, pleated at the waist for more comfort and agility. Soft leather shoes.

It had been years since Leone had seen his friend. He had intended to visit with Charles after the Peterson case was over. Had been looking forward to a little relaxation and the chance to spend time with his dear friend. To Leone, Charles appeared the same other than a slight graying at the temples.

Charles had not noticed Leone as he inquired, breathlessly. "Yes, Della. What is it?"

Della Anderson pointed in the direction behind him. "There is someone here to see you."

Charles spun around, then exclaimed: "Leone! How wonderful to see you mon ami!" They each shook hands a moment until McLane pulled his friend into a warm embrace. Della simply stood at her desk, gawking, thinking she had never seen her boss so effusive.

"Please," Charles continued as he moved easily from the hug to slide his arm around Leone's shoulder. "Step into my office. It has been too many years!"

Charles poured them both a small glass of whiskey. After seating his guest across from him, Charles settled into the leather chair behind his large, cluttered desk. "As you can see my old friend I am still neglectful when it comes to doing the paperwork." He laughed as he pushed a stack of forms aside. "You were always the one to meticulously keep everything in order."

Leone smiled. It was true. Not matter how many times he had explained to his friend the importance of an exact filing system, Charles steadfastly ignored the advise. Time would be wasted handling such trivial things. There was too much to be done with other tasks, was his reasoning.

"You seem to have changed little," Leone offered in his most complimentary tone.

"Were that it were true," Charles stated almost sadly. "So, mon ami, tell me how your case went. Is Peterson going to gain custody of the child? Are you going to be able to spend a few days with us now that you have finished?"

Leone stared at the amber liquid in his glass, then took a sip. "I guess you have not heard. I resigned from Peterson's case." The words carried the bite of the liquor he had just ingested.

"Resigned? But why? I know it was a little out of your realm of expertise as an industrial attorney. Still, the case seemed cut and dried."

"Tell me, Charles, what do you know of the man John Fern and the girl Nis?" Inside, Leone was fighting his nervousness. Though this was a dear friend whom he trusted, he must be careful. He needed to obtain any and all information he could without alarming anyone. He did not want anything to leak back to John Fern. Not until he learned the whole story.

Charles seemed a little taken aback by the question. "Oh, not much I am afraid. I only settled in this area three years ago."

"You must have learned something about these people in that time," Leone insisted. Then, on a lighter note: "I know you. After 10 minutes at a social you knew every female at the party. You even knew if she were happily married, unmarried or married yet available!"

"True, but that was pleasure, and a very long time ago my friend. This is business." He smiled, nonetheless, at Leone's interpretation of himself.

"I have been informed that the old man deals in moonshine. And, I might add that he makes a decent living at it."

"Leone, I too, know you. Perhaps I would be better able to help if I knew what you are up to. You, my friend, are not the type to bother yourself in the contraband of illegal alcohol. Prohibition is over therefore I cannot see you standing to make a great deal of money from an old Cajun and his corn water."

"Touche," Leone said. "Oui, mon ami. There is more. That is why I have come to you. I need your assistance." Leone took notice of his friend's use of words, "corn water."

"I will help in any way I can. What is it you are trying to learn?" Charles inquired. Then, as Leone started explaining the unusual event, he paled.

"She is Anna's child, Charles," Leone intoned sternly as he told the story. "For years, we thought her dead. It was easier for all of us, but mostly for Anna. When so much time passed with no demand of ransom, we believed whoever had taken the babe had done so out of malice or wanted a child of their own. I cannot begin to tell you of Anna's pain. It was her only child."

Charles felt as if his heart had stopped. He had met Leone's beautiful sister on several occasions. He knew of the closeness between the two of them. He had telephoned Leone after reading about Anna's baby being kidnapped and offered his condolences.

He, like so many others, had eventually forgotten about the traumatic event and gone on with his life. Now, the memory of his sadness for his friends of so many years ago knotted his stomach. His mind drifted back to the conversation he and his son, Sly, had had after his upsetting meeting with Peterson.

"Dad, we were drunk! None of us meant to hurt the girl! We were just celebrating our graduation with the old man's corn water. I don't even remember who came up with the idea in the first place." That was Sly's story.

Charles had wanted to believe his son. Wanted and try to understand why Sly would, or even could participate in such a cruel act.

"What part did you play? Tell me honestly Sly for I am seriously contemplating calling in the authorities in this matter!"

"Dad," Sly almost smiled, "We have done nothing wrong. Everyone knows about Uncle John and the girl. No law will step in to protect those kind of people! They are nothing but common trash!"

Charles had bolted from his high-back, leather chair, and before he could realize what he was doing, back-handed Sly hard across his cheek and mouth. Never before had he laid a hand on his son in any matter. But then, he had never been so angry either.

Sly moaned, covering his mouth with his hand as the blood began to ooze through his fingers. Shocked at his father's behavior he remained motionless. Waiting...

"You will tell me everything about that night!" Charles ranted. "I will be the judge of what you did to that girl. She is, whether rich or poor, still a human being!" He then reached and grabbed Sly by the collar, pulling him close. Eye to eye they met, for Sly was every bit the height of his father. "Start talking!" Charles ordered, his face flushed with anger. "No lies.

93

For I swear to you, you will, one way or another, pay for what you have done."

It was the hardest thing Charles could ever remember having to tolerate as he sat, listening to Sly's story.

"I swear, Dad, I never touched the girl. Stan had been the only one."

"Charles?" Leone asked, noticing his friend's strange pallor. "Is something wrong?"

Snapping back to the moment, Charles stammered in reply, "No. No, of course not. It is only that the shock of Anna's child living so close, after all these years…"

"You have never see the girl then," Leone smiled in relief.

"No, I have not. But how did you know that I have not?"

"Because, if you had, you would have known, or thought you knew, who she was. She is an exact duplicate of Anna. The same hair, the exact same eyes…"

To be sure, Charles could never forget Anna's eyes. Unlike those of anyone he had ever known. A trait among the women in Leone's family, it had been explained to him.

"She would be beautiful then," Charles spoke softly, composing himself. "I was told the girl was pretty." Then, thinking back, "I was also told that she was…is…"

"Daft?" Leone interjected. "She is not that way at all, I assure you. I believe that she is merely a product of her environment. She is unable to communicate in a language that you and I speak. She is simply ignorant of the ways of the world outside the swamp."

"Yes, of course," Charles answered. His mind was now in a turmoil. As angry as he had been with his son, and disappointed that Sly could behave in such a heartless manner, he was now faced with having to protect that same beloved son. But how? How could he protect Sly from Leone? He felt torn. Torn between his own flesh and blood and a person he had loved and trusted as a brother for so many years.

How far would Leone take this matter? To be sure, Sly had been wrong in his part of the event. Though he claimed not to have actually raped the girl, he admitted he was present during the awful act. He could have intervened, done something! Would Leone be able to understand a young boy's foolishness and be lenient? Would he, himself, be lenient to someone who had hurt his child?

"Do you think I could possibly intrude and stay at your home for a few days?" Leone asked.

"It will not be an intrusion. We have been looking forward to your visit with us. Your room has been awaiting you arrival from the moment we heard of your plans to come here to represent Franklin Peterson," Charles said, truthfully.

"I um...I will have to impose on you and request a vehicle. I will need to be able to move around this area."

"Of course. Consider it done. I will give you directions to the house and call and let Angela know you are coming. You look like you could use a good night's rest!"

"Thank you, Charles. However, there will be time to rest later. Though I had been so looking forward to this visit as a pleasurable respite, it now has turned into a serious situation. I am sorry."

"How is it that the child ended up here in such a remote and dreary environment?" Charles asked, still bewildered by all the unsettling news.

"I am afraid the only person able to answer that is John Fern. Your discretion would be appreciated in this matter. You do understand that the child Franklin Peterson wants so badly is Annissa's child? Anna Bradford's grandson?"

Charles gulped. In an instant, sweat poured from his brow as he said to himself: "Dear God!"

After procuring Leone a company vehicle and given directions to his home, Charles went back into his office. Suddenly he felt old and tired. He struggled with his conscience. Why had he not just come out and explained what he knew? Leone would stop at nothing to rectify what happened to Anna's child and he could not blame him.

Charles had told Della that he was not to be disturbed, and it was well over an hour later before he emerged from his solitude. He knew what must be done. There was no other way. It would be hard on his family, but it was for the best.

Meanwhile, Leone headed toward the small town of Cypress. He was not sure where he would begin, but if this town was like most rural communities, the favorite pastime among the townfolk would be to gossip. Everyone knew everyone. And even if they did not truly know someone they had certainly heard something about them.

Leone spied a bright yellow and blue sign and pulled into a small Sunoco station. Two white pumps stood out front as two elderly men occupied a bench nearby. Glancing down at the dashboard gas meter Leone almost wished it had not read full. That would have given him a good excuse to chat at length with the men. Now, it looked like he would just buy a cold drink, be friendly and be on his way.

"Good day, gentlemen," he offered pleasantly as he climbed out of the car. "Any chance of purchasing a cold soda around here?"

"Be cold sodies in thet drink box yonder," one of the men responded after spitting a dark substance from his mouth on the ground near his feet.

Neither man got up as Leone walked over to a drink box and lifted the lid. Choosing a bottle, he then uncapped it with the opener on the side. He took a long swallow, then said, rhetorically: "Sure is a hot one today."

"Mmmmm," one of them grunted.

"Ye be adriving yonder Mister McLane's auto?"

Of course, that was obvious, Leone thought. The name of the business was painted on the door of the sturdy, red Ford pickup. Still, it was an opening for conversation. "Charles McLane is a friend of mine."

The man who had spoken, spit again. He seemed totally unconcerned and not in the least curious about Leone. But Leone knew different. He had dealt with people in small towns before and knew that before the sun set the whole town would know about a stranger's visit.

"Yes. Just arrived this morning," Leone returned cordially. "McLane is too busy to break from the shipyard, so I thought I would just show myself around."

"Tain't much ta see. Be judging by yer clothes there you be used to a much bigger ta do than ye be afinding round here."

Leone made note of the man's speech. It had a drawl and the Southerner's way of clipping words. It was not, however, the language Annissa used. "Funny, I thought all the people in the area spoke a language ah…ah…Cajun. Yes that's what I was told." He lied.

"Hurmph!" The other man finally spoke up. "Be a lot of people round-abouts do speak Cajun. Not white folks though. Them dang Creoles be what started the mixin' of the blood. Creole be half French and half negro."

Leone thought it strange the way the man made the statement in such a disparaging tone, as if he were of a better class of people purely because his skin was white. If you could consider it white. The man looked to Leone as if he had shied away from water for way too many years.

"Kinda was thinkin', at first sight, ya being that way yerself. Color of ya skin and all." The second one continued. "Course now, can't likely say I ever did see one all gussied up like ya. Most of your kin don't likes to venture in ta town."

Leone dislike the man immediately. Not for his mannerism nor his speech, but clearly for his prejudice.

"I am French," he offered defensively, not caring to stay around them any longer.

Then, the one chewing the tobacco spit again, glanced at his bench partner and said, "Thought so. Same difference."

Leone reached in his pocket and plucked out a nickel. "This should cover my drink," he said curtly, then turned and left. Driving farther into the small town, he fervently prayed that everyone was not like those two. Ignorance could be excused most of the time. But hating someone because they are another race was intolerable as far as Leone was concerned.

Then, thinking of Annissa, his heart ached. Her skin was not truly quite as dark as his and Anna's. But having her arms and face subjected to the sun over the years gave her enough color to have given these narrow-minded people the idea that she was Creole. Half Negro, the man had said bitterly. Hate and bigotry had been Annissa's legacy from these people. He could well imagine how she was scorned if she ever came around them.

Then, continuing in thought, he could visualize why Peterson's son had been attracted to her. Enchantingly beautiful would be the best phrase to describe his niece, Leone decided. Graceful, yet without the proper training in etiquette. She could not know of her ancestry, but felt in his heart his MaMa and GrandMaMa would know joy in the blood-line being so strong. Even raised in poverty, the child carried herself regally.

Perhaps she had found some kindness in the young boy, Stan. Had been lulled into believing he really cared about her. That would explain the pregnancy. How lonely she must have been.

Then, another thought struck him. Charles' son had graduated last year. Charles had told him about Sly's making it into a state college when he had called about helping Peterson. Sly might be able to help more than anyone. Especially if he had known the Peterson boy well.

Excited about this sudden realization, he turned the car around and headed back toward Charles' home. Then, just as quickly, his hopes were dashed. After all, if Charles had known anything about a friendship between the boys he would have said so, wouldn't he? His mind continued to debate the issue. Young boys were not prone to talk very much about their coming and goings.

Either way, Leone was tired. He would just go to Charles' home and try to rest. There was much to do and he had already learned not to involve any type of private investigator. Other than getting a few photographs, there had not been any way in which his own investigator had been able to find out any more information. Except that the local people, when asked about John Fern, claimed to know little of the man. They knew little, that is, except to say: "He makes damn good whiskey!"

The directions to Charles' home were easy enough to follow. Turning off the main highway down a narrow lane canopied by century-old oaks dripping with Spanish moss, then coming to a clearing with a striking two story white stoned mansion standing proudly.

Leone had not even exited the vehicle when an excited Angela came bursting through the door. "There you are!" she exclaimed, throwing her arms around Leone's neck. "Charles called hours ago saying you were coming." She entwined her arm through his and led him back toward the house.

Leone smiled down at her. "You have not changed one bit, I see. Still too much energy!" He chided gently, for Angela had always been full of energy and life. A very petite lady, she was never one to be lazy or discontented.

"How are Lisa and the children? How long can you visit with us? I saw Anna's latest film, she is absolutely gorgeous!"

Leone could not help but laugh at her enthusiasm. Playfully he answered, "Fine. Not sure. I have not had the chance to see it myself."

Angela looked perplexed with him comments then laughed heartily. "Oh, you!"

After entering the home, Leone let out a soft whistle of appreciation as he looked about. "I must say, Angela, with the exception of Charles, you have extraordinary taste! Your home is beautiful!"

She beamed with pride, smiling at Leone's remark about her husband. She knew it was offered in jest for he and Charles were the closest of friends. "Thank you. I have your chambers ready for you and I do think you will be pleased."

An imposing dark-skinned man took Leone's coat and attaché case. "I can shows you to yer room when you are ready, sir."

"Thank you." Leone smiled. "I have a small suitcase in the automobile, as well." The black man nodded politely and left.

"Please join me on the veranda for a glass of lemonade. Or citronade as the local's refer to it,"

Angela said as she ushered Leone over to a pair of large glass doors encased in cypress frames.

"It is how we, the French, refer to such refreshment, as well," Leone offered as he followed.

"I am sure you will fit in quite well in this area, Leone. A good many of the people here still speak French. While Louisiana is certainly a part of our United States, the ancestry of the French is still very much a part of this area."

Leone nodded. "So I am learning. However, my brief tour of the town led me to believe that anyone with such an ancestry is somewhat below the white standards."

"There are still a few who would have all of Louisiana white. Their ignorance of their own land is a shame," she commented, shaking her head.

"Am I to understand that you like the area?"

"I must admit, when Charles came up with the brilliant plan to move here I was concerned. I worried that Sly would not get the proper education and socialization he needed." She talked as she poured two tall glasses of freshly squeezed lemonade. Then, handing one chilled tumbler to Leone, she continued: "But the truth of the matter is we love it here. We have adapted to this life much easier than I had expected."

Leone wanted to badly to intrude on Angela's one-way conversation and ask direct questions about Sly and the possibility he knew something about the Peterson's son. But, he held back. These people were friends. He would not abuse their hospitality by behaving like a lawyer.

Leone and Angela spent the next hour catching up on each other's family. Annissa's name never entered the conversation. Leone felt that Charles would be best at explaining things to his wife.

Later, just as Angela had predicted, Leone was shown to his suite of rooms and was very pleased.

◆ ◆ ◆

When Charles arrived home, a little earlier than normal, Angela kissed her husband on the cheek, saying: "I wondered if you would be coming home early to spend time with Leone. You two have not seen each other for such a long time."

"Is he resting?" Charles asked quietly, hopefully.

"Yes. He seemed very tired."

"Angela, we have to talk." Charles' tone took on an air of urgency.

She looked at her husband strangely. "Is something wrong?" Her own words began to tremble with uneasiness.

"I am afraid so. I would rather have never had to talk to you about this, but as it happens, I have no choice." He was now weary of all that was happening around him.

"Charles? What is it?" Angela prodded. She was not accustomed to Charles behaving in this manner. Her motherly instinct soon surfacing, she asked, frantically: "Has something happened to Sly?"

Charles' refusal to answer that most important question only heightened Angela's fear as he continued: "Come. Let's walk down by the water." Charles prayed the crisp air would calm him as he explained to his gentle wife what had happened and was still yet to happen.

Leone had rested for a while. Though, normally, he would never lie down during the daylight hours, he was tired. He had wanted to be able to visit with Angela and Charles a bit before getting totally engrossed in solving Annissa's case. But he also knew that if he pressed on he likely would collapse from exhaustion.

He knew, too, he was up against a very powerful foe in Franklin Peterson. Still, he felt confident that he could prove Annissa's background and ancestry and that she, and the child, would benefit from the support of her true family. Then, there would be no sufficient reason for removing her child from her custody.

Stretching, he walked over to the balcony. It was a beautiful sight. The ever-so-slight movement of the tide would almost make one think the Gulf of Mexico was merely a large lake rather than the vast body of water that provides equatorial transit between the Atlantic and Pacific oceans.

On the horizon, Leone could see the outline of a shrimp trawler, its outriggers extended down on each side, pulling its nets across the gulf's smooth, sandy bottom.

Charles' estate was an exquisite place indeed. It was located on the shore, yet the manor house was built back far enough to conceal the wide expanse of white sand stretching in both directions as far as the eye could see.

As he admired the immaculately kept lawn and landscaping, Leone caught sight of Charles and Angela as they strolled arm-in-arm toward the gulf. His first thought was that of romance; that this loving couple must walk on the shoreline often. It was only when he glimpsed Angela abruptly pulling away from Charles that he detected something amiss.

Not desiring to intrude on their private moment, Leone turned away and left the balcony. He crossed the plush carpeted room heading directly for the spacious bathroom thinking a warm shower and change of clothing would do him wonders. Later, as he prepared to go downstairs, he could not quite shake the vision of Angela snatching herself away from her husband. She had been angry. It seemed as if she had been screaming at Charles, Leone hoped, sincerely, that his friend's marriage was all right. They had always seemed perfect for each other.

As he reached the bottom of the staircase, Leone was greeted by the dark-skinned man who had helped him earlier. "Mr. Charles ax you ta join him upon your awakening, sir."

"Thank you," Leone replied, following in the servant's footsteps while being ushered to the veranda. Charles was standing at the wooden rail surrounding the porch. Leone's host was staring out at the endless expanse of water. "I apologize for not being awake when you came home," Leone announced. "The bed was just too inviting."

Charles turned to Leone. "I am glad you rested. You did seem weary."

Leone noted the worry in Charles' face, but resisted the urge to pry into his private life. Charles walked over to a white wicker service table and poured two small snifters of 101 proof Wild Turkey.

"Dinner will be late," he said while handing Leone a glass of the potent Kentucky bourbon. "I still remember your preference in spirits."

Leone smiled in agreement. Taking a swallow, he let the warmth of the rich bourbon glide down his throat, then let out a sigh of satisfaction. A small breeze was blowing in off the gulf and the smell of the salty air was exhilarating.

"I do have to compliment you, my friend. You certainly have chosen a beautiful lifestyle here. I will definitely bring Lisa for a visit soon. She would love this place."

"Angela would love having Lisa here for a visit as well. Though we have been here only a few years, I think sometimes Angela feels lonely. Most of the women in the area are not so friendly." Charles commented almost sadly.

"She appears happy enough to me, Charles," Leone said, remembering her cheerful conversation earlier.

Charles seemed not to hear Leone as he explained: "The reason dinner will be late is to give Sly enough time to come home. As I told you earlier, he has enrolled at Louisiana State up in Baton Rouge."

"It will be good seeing him again. I cannot even imagine how grown he must be. I think you would not recognize Robert and Sher as well," Leone replied, referring to his own children.

Charles then turned to face Leone. "I called for him to come home today after you left the office." He sighed deeply, staring down into the amber liquid in his glass. "I owe you an apology, Leone. I…"

Leone could see Charles struggling with what he had to say and was suddenly feeling that it had a lot to do with their conversation at the boatyard.

"I did not tell you all I knew about Anna's daughter, though finding out her identity was quite shocking."

"Tell me," Leone hastened, abandoning his casual mood. "Tell me what you know."

"Before I do, let me explain why I held back earlier. It was because of Sly."

"What does he have to do with this? I was going to ask you if he was a friend of the Peterson boy since they were around the same age."

Charles was having trouble deciding just how much information he should give Leone. So he tired to sidestep the issue altogether, "I want Sly to explain things to you. Things I was not aware of myself until recently. But, to answer your question, yes, Sly and Stan Peterson were close friends."

Unable to stop himself, Leone inquired: "Do you think then that he will be able to enlighten me regarding Annissa and Stan's relationship? Perhaps he knew of Stan's visits with her."

Charles stared at Leone in astonishment. "Relationship?"

"Well, of course! After all, Annissa did have the boy's child. They had to have been seeing each other. My guess is Stan was too ashamed to tell his father he was seeing a backwards Cajun girl from the swamp."

Tears welled up in Charles' eyes as he listened to Leone's theory. God, but how he wished it had been that way. Not the way he was going to have to reveal now. "Leone..." Charles tried meekly to interject.

Leone was so wrapped up in his version of the story and excited now that he had been correct with the assumption that Sly would be of help, he barely heard Charles. Now, turning back to him, he saw the tears in the man' eyes. "Tell me."

"She was raped, mon ami." Charles' words tumbled out.

Anger, such as he had never known, began to boil within the very depths of Leone's soul. The very words he had once entertained, then dismissed, now came back to haunt him. She was raped. It was all he could do to keep from grabbing this man only a few feet away and beating him furiously. Raped? His mind screamed over and over with rage.

"By all that is holy, Charles, she is only a child! Who…Why?…The Peterson boy raped…?" The thought was so unthinkable, Leone could not finish.

"I want Sly to explain that night to you, Leone. That is why he is coming home today."

"He was there?" Leone roared. "If he was, then he can help me. I must return Annissa's child to her. There has been enough taken away from my family. The baby belongs to us!"

By now, Leone was all but screaming and Charles felt as is his heart could burst having to put Leone through this horrible enlightenment. It had been torture just explaining to Angela why Sly was coming home today. He had to tell her all he knew. Sly's involvement as well. Afterward, she had taken off, running to the shore, tears cascading down her lovely face. She had not wanted to believe what Charles had told her about Sly and the rape. There was a mistake. There just had to be!

The sun was setting with a deep red hue on the horizon. Angela still had not come home and Charles kept gazing toward the gulf hoping to see her return before dark. "Angela had not been aware of any of this until today." Charles told Leone in a sad tone.

Leone now knew why she had seemed so upset earlier when he had see them walking. "How long have you known about this, Charles?" Leone insisted. For the first time, he acknowledged disappointment in the friendship he held with the man.

Charles noted the hostility growing in his guest's voice. He could not blame Leone for being angry. "I knew nothing until Peterson invited me to his home after his son's death. I was shocked and hurt to know my son could be a party to such a brutal act. Please Leone! You have to believe me that I never meant to hurt you or anyone! Sly swore to me he had no part in the rape. Only Stan!"

"So, now that you know who the girl is…Now it matters to you?" Leone was disgusted and turned to leave.

"I felt like strangling him!" Charles cried. "I have never laid a hand on my son and I hit him so hard I thought I had broken his jaw! And no," Charles gritted his teeth, saying with renewed firmness: "I did not know who the girl was. It made little difference. Sly should never have been in that situation. He should have been man enough to stop it, even if he had no part in it!"

Charles gripped the railing so tightly as to turn his knuckles white. "I thought about going to the authorities. But it would be, like Sly said, useless. The law enforced by the local authorities we have around this area is all but a joke. A blind eye and a deaf ear would be all that I could hope to receive. That is the way it has been for too many years, especially when it comes to Ol' Uncle John and his corn water. In this parish, with its predominantly Cajun style of life, the corn water is as much a part of their tradition as the "treaters."

Leone felt his anger dissipating somewhat with Charles' every word. Knowing him to have always been a gentle man Leone walked over to Charles and put a supporting arm around his muscular shoulders. "I seem to remember more than a few scrapes we narrowly avoided in our younger years," he consoled. "Perhaps, if we approach our problems with the same tenacity as we did then, we can get through this. For everyone's sake." Then, as an afterthought: "What the heavens is a 'treater'?"

Angela had just started back toward home and stopped to take in the glorious sight of the disappearing sun. She had just been able to get her wits about her after the news Charles had laid upon her and now the tears threatened to spill forth again as she caught sight of Leone embracing her husband on the balcony. She was grateful for the thought of their friendship remaining intact. Charles had explained to her that Leone would have to know everything and that it would be more suitable coming from Sly, himself. But she felt somewhat betrayed by the two men she loved most in the world.

Betrayed by her son, who she thought she knew so well. Never knowing him to be anything but honest with both herself and Charles. Betrayed, as well, that Charles had kept something so important from her.

110

She knew he thought to protect her, but that reasoning was not good enough.

She continued on toward her home still uncertain how they would get through this, this nightmare. Stepping up to join the men a sudden thought struck her. If she thought this was a nightmare, what had that poor young girl thought while being tortured and raped those many months ago. The girl she now knew to be Anna Bradford's daughter, had only been fourteen years old.

Angela suddenly felt ashamed of her selfishness concerning her family. In a way that was still unclear to her, as far as Sly's involvement, her family was partly responsible for what had happened. With that thought, she squared her shoulders. Whatever wrong had been done she would support Charles' decision to make things right. It was the right thing to do.

Late that same evening Sly finally arrived. He sensed immediately this was not the usual homecoming. There were no warm hugs to greet him. Not even from his mother whom he loved so dearly. Instead, he had been instructed by the servant to join the family in the study.

Sly was trembling as he entered the room. Three grim faces turned toward him. Unfriendly faces. He swallowed hard, noticing Mr. DeLeiu standing close to his father. All his father had said was for him to come home. The matter of the girl had resurfaced. And that it was bad. "Mom. Dad. Mr. Deleiu," he greeted, trying to maintain his composure as he walked over to extend his hand to his father's oldest friend.

Leone was taken aback by Sly. He was a very good-looking young man. Clean shaven. At least six feet tall and slim. He had his mother's soft bright eyes and his father's muscular build. He had not see Sly in more than 10 years and now felt he was looking at a stranger, not the boy he had once bounced on his knee. Leone took the offered hand. A part of him wanted to turn down the hand that had offered no help to Annissa and yet the part of him that so loved the young boy's family still wanted to embrace him.

After everyone was seated, Leone chose to remain quiet as Charles began the story of Leone finding Annissa. He saw the young man pale at the realization the girl being discussed was the very same newborn child who had been stolen from the famous actress Anna Bradford so many years earlier.

Hours passed and the wonderful supper that had been prepared went untouched, much to the dismay of the cook. When, finally, all emerged from the study, the butler would later tell others there was no color at all to any of the faces. As if all of them had seen a ghost.

Upstairs, a still shocked Sly lay stretched out on the still made bed. Legs crossed. Arms clasped under his head. As hard as he tried, he could not shake away the memories. Had not been able to since the night it happened.

Oh sure, he had joined in with Fred's banter of laughingly telling Stan he was making too much of the deal. Somehow, he even convinced himself that they had done nothing wrong. Not really. And he had not let on to anyone that for nights after they had committed the act he had awakened with her cries in his ears. He had not understood what she was saying, the language being so foreign to him. But even in his intoxicated state, he heard her. Knew she was frightened and hurting.

Never would he intentionally hurt anyone. Even if they were poor. If anything, his heart knew, he could have tried to protect her and maybe in his own way, he had.

Sitting up on the side of the bed, once again the scattered moments came back to haunt him. He had been holding the girl's arm. He could remember the damp grass under his hands as he did so. Looking into Stan's eyes he could tell that his friend was barely able to see, much less think. But Fred's voice. So loud. So demanding, seemed to be the rule.

The girl had screamed as Stan penetrated her and somehow Sly's mind became focused enough to know what they were doing was wrong. Trying desperately to think of a way in which to stop the madness, it was the girl who had given him the idea. "She's dead!" He had screamed.

He knew differently because he had noticed how her small arm throbbed with her pulse under his touch. But it was the only thing he could think of at the moment to say. He had to stop the madness. Somehow!

Sly had lived with her screams of torture and the death of a close friend for so long that telling the story tonight had been a relief. Shame and guilt had become a constant companion. So much so that he began trying to study the Cajun language. Unfortunately, Sly found there was little information in the college library on the dialect. After inquiring about the absence of such information he had been told that such a language was not to be recognized. One either spoke correct English or true French.

He wanted to understand the words the young girl had squealed in anguish that night. In many ways, he knew he was just like Stan. He, too, was tortured by the beautiful young girl. She had been so helpless. So small. And her beautiful, clear eyes would forever haunt him in his dreams.

It was tonight that Sly's parents learned that their son's college major would not be in business, as they had always believed. It would be in medicine. "In healing." He had told them all with tears in his eyes. "I have to give something back."

That night, in the McLane household, there was suddenly hope. In one day, all dreams and trust and love between two parents and their child had been usurped. Yet, at the end of a very long and torturous day, there was a small light glimmering at the end of a long, dark tunnel.

Leone, now once again in his bed chambers, reflected back on the events of the day. He could share the McLanes' optimism. But, mostly, the relief he felt for a family he so loved, was enormous. And, yes, in his own way, Sly had saved Annissa from a worse fate. An event involving any other three young men, celebrating their manhood, could have resulted in Annissa's death.

So, in a strange way, Sly had managed to save a life. Two lives, as it would not turned out. Annissa's and that of her son.

And, as for the father of Annissa's child, well, one would have to be a totally ignorant human being to think of him as insensitive. According to Sly, and what Leone had already learned, the young man had not been able to face what he had done. Had not been able to discuss his problems with his own father. And perhaps, Leone surmised, he was too embarrassed to go to his mother either.

It was all too sad. Yet, in a large way, something miraculous had happened. He had found Annissa.

◆ ◆ ◆

The next morning, Leone could not say that he was very much more rested. He had tossed and turned throughout most of the night and though his body screamed for rest, his mind was too busy planning ahead. At least now he had more evidence to sustain him when he fought for Annissa's rights as a mother.

Descending the stairs, the aroma of ham and eggs and fresh-baked bread attacked his nostrils. Lord, but he was hungry! He had not eaten a bite all the day before. Entering the small breakfast nook he was pleased to see Charles and Angela sitting at the table.

"Good morning!" He said. His weariness gave way to a cheerful tone.

Charles had been holding up a newspaper and put it down. "Good morning, Leone. I would have hoped you would sleep a little while longer this morning."

Leone smiled at Angela. He noticed the small, swollen bags under her eyes and felt she had not rested well either. "I am afraid I have much to do today. And my selfish belly threatens to cause major bodily harm if I do not listen to it!"

Angela smiled at that. "Breakfast is laid out there on the server or I can get it for you if you wish."

"Thank you, no. You would not do this poor man's stomach justice, judging by the small portions on your plate."

She laughed a little as Charles asked: "What happens now, Leone?" His concern for his son was clearly visible.

Leone piled his plate full with liberal amounts of scrambled eggs country ham and fried brown potatoes. Reaching for toast and spooning home-made jelly on the side of his plate, he answered over his shoulder. "I understand your concern, Charles. However, my main objective now is to make sure Franklin Peterson has no rights to Annissa's child. "And", he continued as he put his plate on the table before him: "Thanks to Sly, I now have some ammunition. Peterson may or may not know of the rape, but either way, he stands no chance in a custody suit. Not now."

"Will you need Sly's testimony? Will he go to jail?" Angela asked.

"I don't think it will go that far. I doubt very seriously if Peterson wants his son's name blackened. And believe me, should it come to that, I would make sure the story headlined every paper from coast to coast!"

Charles and Angela looked at each other. They knew Leone was a man of his word. God help Franklin Peterson should he attempt to fight back!

"Should it come to pass that the story must be revealed, I promise you what Sly did was enough to keep him from being convicted. As far as I am concerned, in his own way he managed to help Annissa."

"What are your plans today?" Charles asked, his shoulders slumping with relief at Leone's words.

"I plan to go back to Baton Rouge. Child services has the baby. I will petition the judge to reopen the case. Only this time I will be representing the mother."

"I am going with you," Charles proclaimed, having already made up his mind earlier. When Leone looked to protest, Charles said adamantly: "I will not be denied. Our family is part of the reason this has happened and I plan to help in whatever way I can."

Then Angela spoke up. "I have only met Janie Peterson on a few occasions, but I am sure I could visit with her. She does not appear to be as ruthless as her husband. Perhaps once she understands the circumstances surrounding the baby she will not want to hurt Annissa. Franklin probably is aware of what happened that night, but I doubt Janie knows."

Leone listened patiently to Angela, then said: "I appreciate what you would like to do, but by talking to Franklin's wife you might alarm him enough to do something drastic. If what you say about the woman is true, then it seems that there will be more hearts broken before this is to end."

Chapter Six

The courthouse was the first stop for Leone and Charles in Baton Rouge. Leone had not bothered to make an appointment and was very surprised when a secretary announced that Judge Oliver would see him. He, with Charles in tow, entered the small, but opulent judge's chamber he had visited only days before. Though, to Leone, it had seemed like weeks.

Judge Samuel Oliver was facing the window behind his desk still wearing his robe. "Judge Oliver?" Leone asked.

Samuel Oliver did not turn around. Instead, he seemed unaware of their presence for a long moment. Then he spoke, as if he were talking through the window to the people below, walking to and fro on the sidewalks. "It is a sad thing when a man struggles for so long to achieve things he thought would serve him in his golden years. Then, to find out that something he had done along his chosen path, designed to help him toward his destination, would one day be the very thing to take it all away."

Leone and Charles looked to each other, each conveying their mutual lack of understanding? "Sir?" Leone queried.

"You are here about the child?" Samuel Oliver asked, finally turning to face them.

"Yes, your honor. I am." Leone answered, taking in the hollow look in the man's eyes. "This is Charles McLane."

Judge Oliver paid no heed to the introduction. He spoke directly to Leone: "I tried to explain to Franklin.

118

He would not listen to me. I have known the man for many years, you see. I thought I could make him listen to reason. But since his son's death he has behaved like a wild man."

Leone listened patiently to the judge, then suddenly felt a cold chill race up his spine. "What are you trying to say?" In an instant, the thought of Annissa's child being harmed frightened him, horribly.

"He came here the afternoon of the hearing demanding to know what you were up to. Though at the time, you had no substantial proof of your assertion that the girl was Anna Bradford's daughter, I still wanted to give you the benefit of the doubt." Samuel wiped his forehead with a shaky hand. "I truly have always tried to an honest and fair judge."

"What happened?" This time, it was Charles who spoke up. He was now as agitated as his dear friend. It was then that Judge Oliver finally noticed him.

"Who did you say he was?" The judge asked Leone.

"Never mind, sir. What the hell are you trying to tell us? What has Peterson done?" Leone was beginning to fume.

"There was never a birth certificate for the child," Samuel said leaning back heavily in his chair.

"Go on." Leone's mind worked frantically, trying to remain calm enough to understand.

"Frank brought in a blank birth certificate and I...I signed it, making it an official record of the child's birth. It proclaims Franklin and Janie Peterson, mother and father."

Leone's anger toward the man was all-consuming. What the judge had done was illegal, but now it would become almost impossible to disprove the child's true parentage. "My God, man!" Leone roared. He had been standing, but now collapsed into a chair.

Charles had been listening and trying to understand the consequences of what had transpired. Then he said to the pale judge, demandingly: "You did this! You will undo it!"

Leone, almost speaking in a whisper, then interjected: "Why would you do such a thing?"

"My friendship with Frank goes back a long way. He threatened to blackmail me with something we…"

"Why are you telling us now?" Leone demanded, his voice booming through the chamber door to the receptionist's office on the other side. "You know as well as I that with the legal document now proclaiming the Peterson's to be the natural parents of the boy, there would be almost no way in hell to prove differently."

Leone was prepared to fight with anything it took to return Annissa's child back to her. To see his loving sister smile again with life renewed. And yet, here was another obstacle thrown in his way. One he might not have had a chance to deal with fairly, except that the judge chose to speak the truth. Why?

It was a moment before Samuel spoke. His eyes seemed to mist over as he said: "I have long been an admirer of Anna Bradford. When her child had been taken from the hospital, I was one of the detectives on the case. For month after month I tried to find even the smallest of leads to help solve her case. I stood by her bed in the hospital room, questioning her. She was the most beautiful woman I had ever laid eyes upon. Her tears haunted me for many years thereafter. Those eyes...Those beautiful eyes, so full of pain. Begging me to find her baby girl..."

Charles and Leone both listened intently, poised on the edge of their chairs. The man was hurting inside. And Leone, surprised to find out Oliver had worked the case, knew some of the guilt he carried.

"The day of the trial," Samuel Oliver continued, "The girl seemed to strike a nerve in me. I, too, thinking her to be unfit to raise a child in squalor, thought Franklin's interest was for the best." Then he looked at Leone. "It was only after you told me who you thought the girl was that I began to remember Anna Bradford's face. I had buried the memories so deep. I had felt like a failure in my position. But one look at the girl's face and with what you had suggested who she might be, I knew. I knew she was the infant I had searched for all those many years. She could be no other."

"Yet, you signed the birth certificate," Charles assailed, still wanting to hurt the man for compounding on the trouble they faced.

"Franklin threatened to ruin me. I was not thinking clearly at the time. A part of me did not want to believe what you had said about the child being Anna Bradford's, so I thought it would be safer just to go along with Franklin's demands." Samuel Oliver started taking off his robe as he continued speaking. "Later, alone with my own thoughts, I began to see the resemblance between the girl and her mother. I knew what I had done was wrong. I knew somehow I would have to rectify this matter."

"So, what do we do now?" Leone asked, relieved that the man's honor might prevail to help them all.

"I have already written to the state Supreme Court tendering my resignation and asserting the need to annul the child's birth certificate." He hung the heavy black robe on a peg and stroked it gently, lovingly. "I am no longer fit to wear this garment. If it means the returning of the lost child I so fervently sought so many years ago, then I gladly relinquish it."

"Can you give me some power to have the proper authorities release Annissa's child into my custody?" Leone was quickly wanting this nightmare to come to an end.

"I can authorize a document. But I am afraid Franklin has already taken him."

"What?" Charles almost screamed. "How could he? How can we get him to release the boy now?"

Leone had been in a deep state thinking about what now confronted them. Quietly, he said: "There is only one person who can finish this now. One person who can get the answers and maybe some justification for all of us."

Charles looked at Leone's solemn face. "Who?"

◆ ◆ ◆

THREE DAYS LATER...

The long, black Cadillac limousine drove slowly down the dirt path, deeper and deeper into the swamp. As it came into a clearing, a tall, overly thin man wearing faded and torn overalls stood up from his rocker. He spat a glob of dark liquid from his mouth and squinted his eyes against the bright sunlight in an effort to see who had come this early in the morn for his corn water.

He watched as the driver, wearing a dark uniform akin to one worn by a pilot, stepped out from the driver's side door. He marched around the rear of the highly-polished automobile and mechanically opened the back passenger door. He stood erect like a soldier as he held the door open.

A slim woman emerged, dressed totally in black, with a black veil over her face. For a moment she just stood taking in the sights around her. Then she started, purposely toward him. Her walk was as regal as anything John Fern had ever seen.

Anna, her insides trembling at the thought of her child being brought up in such a vile atmosphere, continued toward the man. She chose to speak her native language just to see if the man understood. "Par le vous Francais?"

John eyed the woman suspiciously, then answered her in the language she had chosen. "Oui. What can I do for you?"

His French was very good. Why had Annissa not picked up on it? She then reverted to English. "You are French, then?"

"No. My Pa, he be French. My ma she be Creole." John was not sure why he was even answering this stately, yet intrusive woman.

Anna, noticing how his English left a lot to be desired, slowly lifted the dark veil from her face. The man paled and started to step backward. "Do you know who I am?"

He was ill-prepared for the woman bravely standing before him. He knew who she was, though not by name. He had seen that face, only much younger, many times. "Whatcha want?" He asked shakily.

"Answers," She replied stoically.

John wiped the moisture from his upper lip. His mind frantically searched for a way out of this confrontation. He had been silently praying that somehow all of this was finished. The girl had been taken along with her babe. He had learned that Peterson now had custody of the wee one and Nis had been taken by the authorities.

Though he missed the girl's presence at times, he was glad to know it was over. Or so he had thought. "I didna take ye bebe." He answered truthfully. Though he wondered why.

"Tell me," she said quietly, yet with authority.

Felix sat, unnoticed, in the automobile. He could not speak French and was relieved when they had converted back to English. He watched Anna's every move intently. He had had one hell of a time convincing her to let him come along. He wanted to make sure no harm came to her. Now, as he watched, the man appeared to be willing to talk to her.

"Would it that I could have, I woulduv gotten ya bebe back to ya after the accident and all," John told Anna.

"What accident?" Anna was lost, but was determined to put the pieces of her family's puzzle together.

"Twerent me but my sister, ya see. She went and got herself tied up with some half-wit. He be the one come up with the idea. Then, next thing I knowed was they were here wit a bebe. She made me promise to keep after the wee one fer a few days and…" Here he shrugged his shoulders. "Well, they never came back."

Anna listened. Then asked: "Where are they? Why have you kept my daughter from me all these years?"

"Dead. They died in one of those automobile crashes. Still never knew all the details of the happenin." Memories flooded back. Memories that had been buried for so long. He had loved his beautiful sister and though their parents had died leaving them with nothing but the land, the shanty and the knowhow to make the corn water, they had been doing well. That was until she hooked up with that fancy dressed foreigner.

John had disliked the man from the beginning. He was greedy. Always bragging. "No back-breaking work for me," he would say. "I am going to find the easy way to make money."

Ol' John's thoughts came back to the present as he faced the beautiful woman before him. "Never did cotton to what my sister saw in the dang fool. Maybe it was her chance to get out. Go somewhere. Don't know." He spat again.

Anna ignored his spitting and forged on. "Am I to believe you were forced to keep her?"

"They brought the wee one here claiming they would be back in two days. I didna want no part of their doings and told them so."

"You took care of the baby then?" Anna asked. The man looked unkept and sickly. Not like someone who would know how to care for an infant.

"Yes," he responded. Then, seeing the disbelieving look on her face, he added: "Had some sperience in the care of my sister."

"You could have let the authorities know. You could have..." Her voice trailed off, starting to crack with emotion.

"No police around. I had not long got out of the army. Escape would be a choicier word."

"You ran away?" She prodded, trying to understand why, if the kidnapping had been botched, he had not done the right thing by returning Annissa to her.

"Not my war, Ma'am. Never was. Was thinking to get a new way of life for myself. Couldn't take the killing. Knew if I tried to give the bebe back I would be found out. Also knew that somehow I be blamed for it."

"So, you kept her."

"Did the best I could. Always sends her away from the house when buyers come. Did not know what had happened until I noticed her swollen belly one day."

"My God!" Anna unconsciously swore: "You are nothing but a heathen! You had no right to keep my child from me! You and any other's involved will pay for what you have done!" Tears welled up in her eyes and she felt Felix's hands on her shoulder. She had not even known he had gotten out to stand beside her.

John Fern had noticed the man as he came to stand with the woman. "Ya have Nis now?" John asked hopefully.

Anna thought how sluggish his English was compared to his French. "Yes. Yes, I do."

He spat again. "Good. Then it be no use to ya to try to punish me now. Too late." With that he spat once more and Anna then noticed that what the old man was spitting was not tobacco, but his own blood.

She understood his meaning and watched as he slowly disappeared into the thick, dark cypress trees. "He is dying." She said aloud, yet without pity.

"Come," Felix coaxed, softly leading her back to the awaiting limousine.

Anna turned for one more look at the dwelling in which Annissa had lived for 15 years. Years she had lived and survived in the hostile environment never knowing any other existence. All the while, Anna had resigned herself to a lonely, hollow life. And all for what? For some greedy couple to have enough money to live an easy life? Were they so ignorant as to know there was no such thing?

John made his way deep into the swamp. It was a path well worn by his feet and his father's feet before him. The woman had been the most beautiful thing he had ever seen. Her eyes had been the same as those of Nis. Never had he thought to see anyone with those strange, colorless eyes. He had at times thought the girl child was hexed to have been given eyes of no color. Now he understood their origin.

Having never owned a television nor set foot in a movie theater, he could not know of Anna's fame. He did, however, think to know royalty, as best one could imagine. And the woman had definitely carried herself as though she were royalty! No wonder his sister thought to become rich beyond their means. Nis must be a princess.

127

He sat beside the bubbling barrel and stirred the fire beneath it. The treater had told him just last week his time was almost up. Somehow it made his spirit lighter telling the woman about the girl. Though he would never have harmed the girl child, he had been forced to protect himself. The dialect she spoke was for protection of her as well as him. The less anyone knew about them the better off they were, was his thinking.

The world had changed greatly since his mother and father had lived carefree days here in Louisiana.

They had lived happily. Choosing not to explore the other means of living, such as the fisheries or the fur trading in the area. The corn water's selling and trading, supplied all the necessities of a simple life for them. They believed their elixir, be it used for medicinal purpose, gout, even epilepsy would be a more profitable trade. Soon, however, the people in the area, especially the women, shunned the Fern's, claiming that the clear, potent corn water was the devil's elixir.

John's parents cared little that they were ostracized. They had never been part of the intertwined families. Never choosing to participate in the La veille, the custom of nightly visits to each other's homes to talk and socialize. Though they were not accepted by the locals on a social level, no one seemed to want to delve into the question of why the Fern's chosen business flourished so.

Anna was solemn as the car headed back down the narrow dirt path. Felix chose to remain quiet as well. She would speak when she was ready.

Then, Felix thought to himself about how they had come to be here in this desolate place. Leone, it seemed, had been correct in his assumption that only Anna's presence could now make a difference. She would be the only one who would be able to get to the truth.

All the questioning of people, the hiring of investigators would take months. Whereas, Leone truly believed, Anna's strength and courage to face these people would be their undoing. It was one thing to answer a stranger when they asked threatening questions; it was quite another to face your opponent. Especially when your opponent was Anna Bradford!

Felix knew they would not be going back to the McLane's home just yet—the home where he, Anna and Annissa had met Leone and agreed to stay. There was one more stop to make, and judging by the tilt of Anna's chin and her shoulders squared to do battle, this would be her day!

◆ ◆ ◆

Dee Peterson looked out her bedroom window with its view of the garden. She watched as her mother sat on one of the concrete benches, smiling at the golden-haired child playing on a blanket that had been spread over the grass. She had never felt so alone in her life.

It had been hard on her when Stan had died and watching her mother fall into such a deep depression. She had tried each and every day to sit by her mother's bedside. Aching to bring her out of her despair. Time would be the answer, the doctor had assured Dee and she had been forced to accept that fact. At least it offered hope to her young mind.

But that was before. Before her father came bustling through the door, running upstairs to her mother's room, a small child in his arms. Dee had followed her excited father and stared open-mouthed at the scene that met her eyes.

Her mother was sitting-up, pillows supporting her. The drapes were pulled open allowing the first rays of sunlight into the room in several weeks. Her father saying: "This is your surprise!"

Janie looked at the beautiful golden child then back to Franklin, still a little groggy, she said: "I don't understand, Frank. What surprise? Who's child is this?"

Franklin placed the child on the bed next to her. His face was alive with pure pleasure. "This is Rand. This is Stan's son!"

Janie put her hand over her mouth to still the sob. Her eyes took in the beautiful boy. His hair was light with gold streaks, and his eyes were a soft brown. Yes, she thought to herself, this is Stan's son. She reached for him and cooed as she kissed his cherub face. "This is a miracle!" she exclaimed. Then, "Where is his mother? I would like to meet her. Do we know her?"

Franklin smiled. His P.J. had actually come back to life! Just as he had thought. "Now, now, dear. There is plenty of time for explanations later. For right now, I just want you to hold you new grandson."

Janie, still under the influence of the heavy medications, did not have the strength to protest or push further into the matter. Later then, she told herself, holding the child close in her arms.

Dee had turned away in shock. Automatically, she made her way to her room where she locked herself in. There were no tears to shed for they had all been spent on the loss of her brother and the alienation of her family. Since Stan's death her parents had seemed to forget about her very existence. And now, another dagger had been twisted into her young heart as Stan almost seemed to reach out from the grave. Through this child.

Her mother had grown stronger each day as Dee had grown more solemn. She had ventured out of her room several times only to have gone unnoticed. So wrapped up in Rand, as her parents were.

Her appetite had completely abandoned her as she became almost reed thin. The darkness under her eyes gave her an almost haunting appearance.

The servants watched the happenings in the once powerfully happy family and whispered sadly amongst themselves. They understood the grief the Peterson's felt at the loss of their son, but they could not understand the lack of love displayed toward their only daughter. And now that Stan's child had entered the picture, mysteriously, it was as if they had never had a daughter.

Now, as Dee watched her mother playing with the robust child and listening to their laughter, she started to turn away. It was in that instant she noticed the long, shiny, prestigious automobile pull up in the drive. Janie saw it as well and called to one of the servants to come and put Rand down for his nap.

Dee had opened her window slightly. It had been a long time since there had been a visitor to their home. She watched as a woman emerged, dressed elegantly in black.

"Hello!" Janie greeted from the garden and the darkly clad woman turned in that direction. "Can I help you?"

Anna watched as the woman strode toward her. She remained quiet and motionless taking in what she thought to be her enemy. Janie Peterson was rather tall and thin, but she carried herself well, Anna surmised. Her face showed tender eyes, though gaunt, and an easy smile.

"Hello." Anna responded, unsmiling, as the woman came to stand in front of her. "Are you Mrs. Franklin Peterson?"

"Well, yes. Yes I am. And you are?" Janie was still smiling, unable to make out the face under the dark mesh. Concern was clearly written on her own.

Anna pulled the dark veil from over her face. "My name is Anna Bradford." Her introduction quite curt.

Janie stared at the beautiful woman, though dressed exquisitely, she struggled with the name. When she finally realized who Anna Bradford was, her first instinct was to actually drop deep into a curtsy. Then, trying to gather her composure, she said: "Mrs. Bradford! What an honor!"

Anna noticed the woman as she began to twist her hands nervously. "Would your husband by any chance be home?" Anna inquired. It was not an act for her to stand there like a queen as if she were speaking to a servant, it came quite naturally.

Janie was clearly shaken and confused that such a famous woman would be at her home asking about Franklin. "N…No. He is not. However if you would like to come into our home and…"

"When do you expect him?" Anna asked briskly.

"This afternoon." Janie stumbled. "Is there something I might help you with?" Though she knew very little about the real estate business, she certainly would not want to offend such a famous woman as this. Perhaps she could just detain her until Frank came home. He was quite used to dealing with celebrities.

At first, Anna had no intentions of doing battle with the woman. She felt, as she studied Franklin's wife, that she was a gentle person. Still, she and Annissa had suffered enough at the hands of others. Though she thought it would be better if she chose to return when Franklin Peterson came home, she now thought differently.

Anna's heart sought vengeance for herself, Annissa and now Tan. Still, she felt herself melt a small bit. She would give this woman one chance. "I will explain this to you and I will give your family one chance to save yourselves. But only one!"

Janie felt her knees weaken as the woman spoke. One chance? "What is it you want from us, Mrs. Bradford?"

"You have my grandson. If you will be so kind to relay a message to your husband. He has but one day to give the child back to us. If not, then, Mrs. Peterson I do assure you that I will stop at nothing to destroy your family." Her voice was dead calm.

Janie's face instantly drained of color as she realized that the famous woman was speaking about Rand. "But you don't understand! The child is…was my son's child. My son is dead!

Anna had started to pull the veil back over her face and halted. "Your son brutally raped my daughter! The child is the result of your son's attack upon my fourteen year old child! As I said…" She gritted her teeth, and took a deep breath: "One day to return the child or you shall all pay dearly!" Anna finished pulling the veil down and turned away from the shaken woman. Then, speaking coldly over her shoulder, she added: "We are staying with the McLanes. We will be expecting you."

Janie stood frozen to the spot and watched the limousine as it drove out of sight. Though still weak from time spent bedridden, something in her began to fume. She walked slowly back to the bench she had been sitting upon earlier while watching Rand as he played.

A small hand came to rest on Janie's shoulder and she turned to see her daughter, Dee. She patted the comforting hand, then pulled Dee around to join her on the bench.

Dee had overheard the entire conversation and was dumb-founded to hear the woman say that Stan had raped her daughter. Not Stan! Dee thought. For even though her parent's had always seemed to adore him over everyone else, including herself, Stan was not a mean person.

Dee recalled many of the times she would rankle him trying to get him angry enough to strike her. To do something so that she could draw some of the attention away from her saintly brother and have more focus on herself. All her efforts were to no avail. Stan was a gentle boy. Always had been. She could not believe the things the woman was saying to her mother.

And, though she was angry with her locking her out of her and her father's world after Stan's death, she could not bear the stricken look that had come over her mother's face. She had rushed down the stairs after the beautiful woman had gotten back into her luxurious limousine.

"Mother?" Dee cried out in her childlike manner.

Janie looked at her daughter to reassure her that everything would be all right, then cried alarmingly: "Dee! Are you ill?" Then, not waiting for a response, she put her hand to Dee's brow. "My heaven's child, but you have a fever! How long have you been sick?"

Janie was shocked at Dee's appearance and true guilt fell over her as if someone had thrown her into a river of frozen water. "What have I done to you?!"

Dee was suddenly pulled tightly into her mother's arms being kissed softly on the forehead and for the first time in a very long time, feeling loved again.

Janie held her too thin daughter, rocking her gently in her arms. As she did so, she thought of all Anna Bradford had told her and many things began to fall in place.

Though she had often been reassured by many around her that Stan's death was not a suicide, Janie had known the truth in her heart. She had watched as Stan slowly sank into some deep well of grief. She had been helpless in trying to find out what was so troubling to her son. But no, she thought again, tightening her hold on Dee. She could have done more. She had, like so many times before, simply sat back allowing Frank to handle the situation.

Now, she felt, she knew the truth. Though she did not know the events that could have possibly led Stan to perform such a cruel deed. Did not know how Stan even came to know Anna Bradford's daughter. And why was such a well know person as Anna Bradford staying with the McLanes?

Franklin must have known more than he had said. Anger began to grow in the pit of her stomach. Anger that he could treat her as if she were an ignorant child! A senseless human being! But no more, she vowed. Never again would she allow her husband to rule her life. She knew that she was not a glamorous beauty and had been lovingly teased by her family as being Plain Jane. Thus, her nickname P.J. And many years back she was content with her choice of marriage to the tall, handsome, Franklin Peterson. Then, shortly after Dee had been born, she had found a letter addressed to her husband and knew he had not remained faithful to their marriage vows.

But Janie now had the responsibility to her two children. So she took the back seat to her husband, allowing him to live as he chose. She, in turn, devoted her life to her children. Frank had always scorned her for molly-coddling them, as he put it. But they were the only people in her life she truly loved.

Stan's death would always be hard for her to accept. But maybe now, having a little more understanding why he had been suffering so, she could begin to heal.

Franklin's insensitivity to people around him was only made clearer to her as she thought of him taking the girl's baby from her. How she must have suffered. He had lied!

"Stan was seeing that Old Uncle John's niece." That was how he had explained it to her. "They could not afford to raise the child and came to me after Stan had died. They wanted money, of course. They are greedy people." He went on. "I agreed to pay whatever they wanted and now the child is legally ours!"

Janie had thought it so sad that a mother would sell her child. But Franklin had explained that that was the kind of people they were. She and Franklin had moved to Louisiana soon after their marriage and through the years Janie had learned of its people. She had always been amazed at the culture in which they still chose to live. Including a language that was their's alone. But to her, they had always seemed to bear a great deal of pride.

The way in which Franklin had described John Fern with his corn water moonshine struck Janie as odd. For the people in the area seemed more family-oriented in her opinion. Nonetheless, here was the child. And certainly, she knew, it was Stan's child.

"Come with me, darling," she now said to Dee. "You are going straight to bed. I will send for the doctor." Then she put Dee's small face between her hands and cried: "I never meant to hurt you. There is no excuse for the way you have been ignored. But I promise you this, there will never be another day that I don't thank God for you."

Both were crying as they entered the house. Jack, a long-time servant to the family, met them as they entered. "Iz thez anythin I can do, Mizz Peterson?"

Janie looked into the dark eyes she had known throughout the years and smiled. "Yes, Jack. Would you see that the baby's clothes are packed and readied to leave, and would you please bring the car around. I am in need of your services."

"Yesum," Jack replied, and watched as Janie helped Dee up the stairs. He smiled to himself. Things are sure looking up around here, he thought. And, as far as the new addition to the family, Stan's child, Jack had been quite skeptical about how Mr. Peterson pulled that one off.

He had not been able to pull himself away from the door as the beautiful lady had been talking. Oh, yes. He had heard it all. And it was time to make things right for everyone concerned!

Chapter Seven

Anna stepped out of the vehicle. Her muscles were sore from the mounting tension of the last few days. But she would not have changed a moment of it for all the money in the world! She smiled as she spotted Angela sitting in one of the rockers on the wide porch. She was speaking to Annissa. Not in any language she had been able to understand. But as Angela had explained, after moving to this area she had been so impressed with the people and their culture, she had begun a novel. So, as it turned out, Angela was the only one able to truly converse with Annissa.

Anna walked up the steps, lifting the long dress as she did so. Felix was at her heels.

Both Angela and Annissa jumped up. Annissa, speaking so anxiously in her foreign tongue. "Y'ou est Tan?"

"She is asking about her bebe," Angela translated. Anxious herself for news.

Anna smiled. "I think I could have figured that one out for myself." Then, she looked into her daughter's eyes. "Angela, please tell her we must be a little more patient. For by tomorrow, one way or another, she will have him back in her arms."

Angela repeated Anna's words in the Cajun dialect as Anna watched the pain fall over her daughters eyes. She pulled Annissa close to her. She knew. God, how she knew what she was feeling!

Somehow, even with the language barrier, she and Annissa had managed to get to know each other. Anna had cancelled every appointment and turned down many roles. Nothing was more important to her right now than her family.

Her whole life had changed and she now knew that any work as an actress would take second place. She now had Annissa and a grandchild. She felt almost complete and had hoped feverishly that Seth was able to look down and see their happiness.

Angela watched the two women, so much alike, and smiled. She knew what the love of a child meant and could not imagine how Anna had remained so strong.

When Leone had come up with the brilliant idea of bringing Anna, herself, to help, she had hurriedly removed all photos of Sly. And there were instructions for Sly not to return home until he was contacted to do so. She wanted Annissa to be comfortable. Any reminder of Sly would most certainly bring back horrible memories for the lovely girl. She felt a loss with the absence of Sly's existence in her home. And once again, marveled at Anna's resilience. One day, she hoped to help Annissa understand Sly's role in the rape. But now was not the time.

"I did not know you had returned," Leone exclaimed as he, with Charles in tow, came out on the veranda to join the others. "Tell me," he said excitedly. "What happened?"

Anna looked into her brother's loving eyes, so much like their father's. "It was as you thought, Leone. My presence rattled them all to the core. The man, John Fern, was so taken aback when he saw my face, there was very little urging on my part to get him to speak. His French is very good."

Leone, Charles, Felix and Angela sat in the wicker chairs totally focused on Anna as she relayed John Fern's testimony of the kidnapping.

"And what happened at the Peterson's?" Charles asked quickly, for he had been very concerned about Anna facing Franklin Peterson alone. It had only been Leone's assurance to him that Anna was quite able to handle the situation and that Felix would be going along with her that caused him to sit and wait.

"Franklin Peterson was not yet home. However, his wife was there," Anna said poignantly.

"Did you speak to her?" Angela asked.

"My first inclination was to wait. Come back when her husband was home. I so relished the thought of facing him." As Anna recounted the story, Charles became even more amazed with her courage. "But, the more I thought about it, who better to threaten than a mother herself. Peterson might want to fight this out until the end. But a woman will do whatever it takes to protect her family." Everyone nodded with agreement.

It was getting late and the aroma of a gumbo having been prepared for supper reminded the occupants on the porch of how hungry they each were. Angela had stepped into the house only minutes before, then emerged to announce that supper was ready to be served. It was then, as they each stood to ready themselves for a delicious meal, that Angela noticed the dim lights of a vehicle moving up the lane toward the house.

"Now, who could that be?" Angela wondered aloud, hoping that Sly had not dared to come back home. Not now, she silently prayed.

The gray sedan pulled up to the steps as a dark-skinned man, the driver, emerged. He went around to the other side of the vehicle to open the door for the back seat passenger.

Charles recognized the man immediately as Franklin's butler and suddenly became worried. Then, much to his relief, Janie Peterson stepped out.

"I do so apologize for this late hour," Janie Peterson said to the on-lookers who had gathered on the porch and now stared, mesmerized by the slim, well dressed, woman. Then, turning to Jack, she said, "Would you please retrieve the cases in the trunk?"

Janie never ventured from the open door of the automobile as she took in the faces of the people on the porch. She spied a very young pretty girl, her hair almost touching the wooded planks on the porch. It was dark, save for the lanterns casting the porch in a soft, yellow glow. but she knew who the girl was and Janie spoke directly to her. "I do believe I have something that belongs to you."

Annissa could not understand what the woman was saying and watched, confused as she bent over to retrieve something from the back seat of the car. "Tan!" Annissa screamed, bolting from the porch with lightning speed. She grabbed the babe roughly from the woman's arms as tears fell freely down her soft, young, cheeks. She held the child closely to her bosom as she danced around in circles.

Anna's tears fell unchecked as she watched the scene unfold before her. For a moment, she was lost in memory. It was she, herself, holding Annissa in her arms and dancing from the joy of having her baby returned to her.

Moments passed and only Charles' masculine sob broke the silence. Angela was at her husband's side, immediately putting her arms around him. Leone came to stand beside Anna and he smiled for the very first time since he had found Annissa.

Anna could not clearly see the woman's face and stepped down from the porch. As she approached Janie Peterson she saw, as well, the tears swimming in the woman's eyes. Anna extended her hand to the woman and softly said: "Thank you."

Janie took the woman's hand and held it tightly for a moment. "I did not know about what Stan had done. There are still many questions to be answered."

Anna believed her and read the confusion on her face as she spoke. She did not offer any explanation, however, for she felt this to be something Janie Peterson wanted to do on her own. Maybe even needed to do.

As the sedan pulled away, Anna slowly walked over to Annissa. She had never seen Annissa's child though she wanted desperately to force Janie to turn him over during their morning confrontation. Now, as she put her slender hand on the baby's face she looked into Annissa's eyes and smiled. Her heart was so full of happiness. She looked up into the star-filled sky and spoke aloud.

"Seth. We are fine now. The only thing missing in our lives is you, my darling."

Annissa watched as her mother spoke up to the sky. Whoever was up there, her mother must have loved them dearly, judging by the strange look on her face. Annissa put Tan in Anna's arms. She, too, understood the loss of someone who was loved so dearly. In her own way she was telling Anna that she would share her love in her child with her. She would try to help the woman not to be so lonely anymore.

Anna held the beautiful toddler and smiled at Annissa's display of compassion. "I am the luckiest woman in this world!"

Charles and Angela smiled, too, tears of joy clearly visible in their eyes. Leone almost choked for it was the first time in 15 years he had seen his sister's face so radiant with happiness.

Felix had tried to stand back, tried to remain aloof from the happenings. But, now, he found himself drawn to Anna's side. It was the first time he had ever admitted to himself that he was deeply in love with her. It was not, however, the time to proclaim his affection. But he knew, as he put an arm around her waist, it would not be long.

Anna turned to him and saw the love in his eyes. She smiled, contentedly.

◆ ◆ ◆

Dusk was setting in as Franklin Peterson arrived home. His driver had let him off at the entrance and left to park the car. The first thing he noticed was Jack's absence. Frowning, he called aloud for his longtime servant. Then, turning toward the kitchen area, he noticed that there were no preparations for supper. The table had not even been set.

Feeling that something was terribly wrong he took the stairs, two at a time and burst through P.J.'s bedroom door. The bed remained untouched. The room was dark now.

He turned, hurriedly making his way to the nursery P.J. had so painstakingly decorated for Rand. It was empty. The blankets removed from the crib and all the small, colorful array of stuffed animals, gone.

His anger was mounting as he struggled to find an explanation for the emptiness of his home. He spied a dim light glowing beneath the door to Dee's room and thought nothing of bursting in.

Dee had almost fallen asleep when the intruder burst through the doorway. Her mind was hazy from the medicine the doctor had given her, telling her mother that plenty of food and rest was all she needed. Now she strained her eyes to focus on her father, who, standing in the doorway breathing hard, frightened her.

"Where is your mother?!" He asked, angrily. Then, when Dee seemed to be struggling with the answer, he came to stand by her bed. "Answer me! Where is the baby?!"

Dee was so frightened seeing her father in this mad state she could not think. He raised his hand over his head to strike her and she screamed. "No! Stop! She...she took the baby...to give him back to his mother!"

Dee was almost in hysterics as she watched her father. A crazed, wild look came over his face. He roared. "His mother?! Why that damn fool woman! Who in the hell does she think she is doing something like this behind my back!"

Dee listened to his ravings and watched as he bolted back through the door, still swearing. "I'll teach that bitch! After everything I have done for her!" Shaking violently, Dee heard the front door slam and knew he had left the house. Her fear included the thought of him harming her mother if he found her. Dee closed her eyes tightly, silently praying. "Dear, God. Please help stop this madness!"

Franklin, anger controlling his whole body, stormed out to the garage. The keys, as always, were hung on the pegboard just inside the door. He snatched them so violently from the wall he tore the hook away from the board. He sped away from the house so loudly that his driver came running out from his small cottage behind the garage. The driver stood, his face contorted in a mass of confusion, watching the vehicle as it sped away. He had been able to get a quick glance at the man in the car and assured himself that it was Mr. Peterson, himself. He turned around to head back. It was not his place to ask questions, he shrugged.

Franklin drove like a madman barely missing a truck as he came barreling down the road. He was furious that P.J. would do something so incredibly stupid. But there would be time for her later. Right now he had to get Rand back. The child belonged to him and no one was taking him away!

Fred Long was just about to turn the key in the door of the hardware store. It was always his job to close. He heard tires squeal and halted to look out to see where the noise was coming from.

He watched as the speeding car came to a screeching halt in front of him and was startled to see Peterson. "Get in!" the still incensed Peterson ordered.

Fred swallowed nervously, taking in the man's ashen color and the strange look in his eyes. "Sir?"

"Get in! I need you to show me where the girl and her uncle live. There are so many of those damned dirt paths out there I don't want to get lost!" Peterson tried to calm his voice enough so he would not frighten the boy.

Fred quickly locked the door from the outside instead of inside the building as he had originally intended. Something was terribly wrong with Mr. Peterson and Fred certainly was not going to pass up an opportunity to help the man out. Not a man like him!

As the car sped off, rubber tires smoking and spinning in the gravel road, Ned Long came out from the back of the store where they lived. Tying his bed robe around him, he watched as the car sped away. He caught a quick glance of Franklin Peterson's profile. Something was going on with the two of them, but what? Ned was still puzzling over the man's last visit with his son. He knew something had transpired because for days afterward, Fred had constantly pulled money from his pocket. He continually bragged about how he was not going to spend the rest of his life in this "rat hole" as he called it. He said he had bigger plans, but never would say what they were.

He was puzzled why Fred had not at least had the decency to come back into the house and let his family know he was leaving. He tested the door assuring himself that Fred had locked up before scurrying away. Then, shaking his head, he turned to go back to his television set. There was a movie on tonight, starring Anna Bradford, that he certainly did not want to miss! "Hurry Ned! The movie's starting!" His wife called.

Fred held on for dear life, feet straining to the floorboard, hands clutching the dash, as Franklin barreled down the road. He wanted desparately to ask Mr. Peterson why he was in such a hurry, but held back. For whatever reason, the man had enlisted his help. No one else's. Fred smiled. He knew he would receive some sort of gratuity from the man. And the idea of more money in his pocket sure sounded good!

Fred instructed Franklin to turn onto the dirt lane and then sat back for the first time since entering the car. Hell would pay for this man's anger tonight, Fred thought and relished the idea of being a part of the excitement.

As they reached the house, Franklin said: "Damn it all, there is no-one home."

Fred, eager to help, offered: "Well. It's kinda hard to tell. You see. Ol' Uncle John stays back there in the swamp where he makes his brew."

"Which way?" Franklin asked desperately.

Fred pointed in the direction he had seen John emerge the few times he had been here. "That way," Fred said, following closely on the man' heels.

As they walked deeper and deeper into the swamp, Franklin swore at himself for not bringing along a flashlight. As they penetrated the bogs, the trees thickened and the darkness enveloped them.

Fred was beginning to wish he had remained behind as he listened to the man in front of him swearing and cursing. The damp moss on the trees seemed to attack them as they, feet sinking into the moist earth, trudged onward.

The younger of the two was just about to turn back, his fear in this damp darkness starting to override his exhilaration and greed. Then, Franklin yelled: "I see a light! It's a fire!"

The two took a few more steps. Franklin was moving faster and several yards ahead, when Fred heard Franklin swear again. "Damn!" Then, he shrieked: "What the hell?"

Fred strained to find the outline of the man in front of him. He froze, listening to him struggling and fighting something. Fred's feet refused to move one more step forward as he whispered: "Mr. Peterson? Mr. Peterson?"

Franklin's voice now sounded far off to Fred as he heard, "For God's sake, boy! Get your fat ass over here and help me!"

But Fred was frozen to his spot. He listened to the man as he fought something, cursing and screaming. Fear, unlike anything he had ever known caused Fred to start backing up. He was not able to see what it was that now tortured the older man and no amount of money in this world could make him move forward and see.

Eyes misted as if in a fog, Fred somehow groped his way back at the shanty. Thinking to get away with his life intact, he jumped into the car. Christ! No keys! Peterson must have taken them. Fred tore out of the vehicle, leaving the door open as he ran as fast as his short legs could carry him, burdened as they were with his heavy girth.

Meanwhile, Peterson, still swearing and screaming, sank even lower in the enveloping soil. A light shown on his face and he immediately slowed his struggle. "Thank God!" he said, seeing the outline of a man holding a light on him. "Dear heavens man! Don't just stand there like an idiot. Help me out of here!"

The man in silhouette remained motionless as Franklin tried to block the light from his eyes to see who towered above him. He heard the man spit on the ground. Then the shadow spoke. "What be yer reason for a bein' out chere?"

Franklin's body was feeling the numbness from all his struggles. Still his anger ruled as he bellowed to the man: "I want that little bitch!" He fought against the vacuum sucking him in. His anger so evident. "You! You must be her damn uncle. Where are they?"

Ol' John watched the angry man, then spat again. He made no effort to help. "Don't rightly can sez I know of what ye be speakin' bout."

"The girl! Nis! Where is she, damn you!"

John backed away from the man and the pool of quicksand that was about to engulf him. He slowly turned to follow the path the man had forged. He needed to be sure there was no one else around. Could not have that! As he walked away he listened to the man's final tirade.

Ol' John knew of Peterson's fortune, how he had acquired it by selling off the local land and he had heard some of the horror stories about his ruthlessness. How he would stop at nothing to get a prime piece of dirt even if it meant burning the people out, leaving them with nothing. How fitting, John thought, to have the very thing in life that the man had so coveted, consume him. The land. Rich but unforgiving land.

"You son of a bitch! I'll kill all of you! All of you! Do you hear me?" Slowly, Franklin Peterson sank deeper and deeper into the sludge. As his mouth went under, he struggle for air. With his anger, all-consuming as it was, it was not until he realized that he was going to die, that a single thought entered his mind. "Stanley. Sweet, gentle Stanley."

The next morning John Fern found himself face to face with the sheriff. Arthur had received a call from Janie Peterson early in the morning claiming that her husband Franklin had not returned home.

Janie had returned to the house finding a very terrified Dee. After calming her daughter down she then phoned the police station stating that she could not be sure, but had thought that maybe her husband had ventured out for some of the area's famous "corn water". Of course, that was the first place Arthur checked and had found Franklin's automobile sitting in the front yard with the door ajar.

"So, you say you have been in the woods all night?" Arthur asked the man, sitting calmly on the stoop of his porch.

"Did nay come out till hears yore car ablwoin." John said.

Arthur eyed the man suspiciously. Then, over his radio in his patrol car, he heard the dispatcher calling him. "Yes, George. What is it?" He answered, talking into a small, hand held transmitter.

"Just got word from Ned Long that his store was robbed. All the money in his register was taken."

"A break in?" Arthur asked.

"Ah, no sir. He says he thinks it was his son, Fred. Mr. Long says Fred had a key and he last saw him, taking off in a car last night with Franklin Peterson, sir."

Arthur put the transmitter down and once again studied the footprints around Peterson's car. One set of prints headed off down the road. And, studying them, Arthur surmised that whoever it was had not been walking. They had run.

He followed more prints to the edge of the woods. "You didn't hear anything?" He asked Ol' John, this time more sternly.

John coolly shook his head, then spat. "Ain't be aheered nuthin' but frogs a croakin'."

The sheriff scratched under his hat. He felt he knew what had happened here last night. He turned back to John as he headed for his vehicle, saying. "I'll have a truck out today to tow away the vehicle. If you should find anything, how about letting me know, Ya hear?"

"Be done, Sheriff." John answered back and turned to walk into the house.

As Sheriff Arthur Main headed back to town, he told the dispatcher: "See that somebody gets a photo of Fred Long. I do believe he has murdered Franklin Peterson and left the body for the gators." Then, to himself, he said: "Always knew that boy was no good for nothing!

Chapter Eight

CHRISTMAS, 1960

"Oh Leone it is a beautiful home!" Lisa exclaimed as she emerged from the car. She was so excited at the thought of meeting Annissa for the first time. Now as she helped Bob, her son, and Sher, her daughter with the decorated, packages it was all she could do to not run up the steps to Anna's new home.

Anna greeted them warmly as she opened the door. And could not help laughing at the abundance of their gifts. "Lisa! I dare say, have you left anything at all in the stores for other people to purchase?"

Lisa's face reddened a little with embarrassment as she answered: "Well, to tell you the truth, my sister, all of these are for Tan!"

Laughter ensued as Anna took her sister-in-law by the arm. Then, turning to Bob and Sher, their aunt called: "Come. Come meet your cousin."

Leone stood in the doorway of the large room. He watched his family, for the first time ever, complete. His mother and father were surrounded by their children, grandchildren and one plum, rosy-cheeked great grandson.

He knew in his heart, that for so long as he lived, he would always remember this moment. The laughter. The love.

Though it had all come about in such a strange fashion, he contributed full credit to the strong trait in his family. A trait that no one could ever take away. For the strength that had bonded his family for so many years before, and even so now, was the bond of inheritance, in the female family's eyes.

The eyes of Innocence.

THE END

About the Author

Sherry Jo Saunders is a true GRITS (Girl Raised in the South). Born in South Carolina, she spent much of her childhood seated at the foot of her great grandma's rocking chair. She would listen intently and absorb every word of her grandma's extraordinary, exciting tales of days long past.

As she grew older, Sherry gained more knowledge of her native South as she traveled throughout Georgia, Florida and westward to Louisiana and Texas. All along the way, she eagerly sought out the yarn-spinners to learn about the lore of the land.

This quest was the seed of her desire to be an author so she could share these stories with readers far and wide. However, more than wanting to be a novelist, Sherry Jo Saunders hopes to be a great storyteller—keeping true to her great grandma's legacy of imparted lore.